FIGHTING
FOR
DUBLIN

This book is dedicated to my mother,
Noreen Sheehan, and my sisters,
Eileen O'Donoghue and Bernadette McAuliffe,
for all their support and help

FIGHTING FOR DUBLIN

THE BRITISH BATTLE FOR DUBLIN
1919–1921

WILLIAM SHEEHAN

The Collins Press

Published in 2007 by
The Collins Press
West Link Park
Doughcloyne
Wilton
Cork

British Library Cataloguing in Publication Data

Sheehan, William
        The Irish War of Independence, Dublin, 1918-
1921: the official British history
                1. Ireland - History - War of Independence, 1919-1921
                2. Dublin (Ireland : County) - History - 20th century
                I. Title
                941.5'0821

        ISBN-13: 9781905172436

Typesetting: The Collins Press

Font: Hoefler, 11 point

Printed in the UK by Creative Print and Design

Cover images:
Front: Armed British troops on the streets of Dublin during the
War of Independence, courtesy *Evening Herald;*
Back: British troops search for documents in the debris of the
Dublin Custom House, May 1921.

CONTENTS

LIST OF ACRONYMS

APM	ASSISTANT PROVOST MARSHALL
AQMG	ASSISTANT QUARTERMASTER GENERAL
ASC	ARMY SERVICE CORPS
BAOR	BRITISH ARMY OF THE RHINE
BEF	BRITISH EXPEDITIONARY FORCE
BN	BATTALION
CB	COMPANION OF THE BATH
CMA	COMPETENT MILITARY AUTHORITY
CMG	COMPANION OF ST MICHAEL AND ST GEORGE
DAAG	DEPUTY ASSISTANT ADJUTANT GENERAL
DCM	DISTINGUISHED CONDUCT MEDAL
D/D	DUBLIN DISTRICT
DDHQ	DUBLIN DISTRICT HEADQUARTERS
DMP	DUBLIN METROPOLITAN POLICE
DORA	DEFENCE OF THE REALM ACT
DPM	DEPUTY PROVOST MARSHALL
D OF WR	DUKE OF WELLINGTON REGIMENT
DR	DUTIES REGULAR
DSO	DISTINGUISHED SERVICE ORDER
EEF	EGYPTIAN EXPEDITIONARY FORCE
GHQ	GENERAL HEADQUARTERS
GOC	GENERAL OFFICER COMMANDING
GSO	GENERAL STAFF OFFICER
HQ	HEADQUARTERS

IC	IN CHARGE
IR	IRISH REPUBLICAN
IRA	IRISH REPUBLICAN ARMY
MC	MILITARY CROSS
MT	MOTOR TRANSPORT
NDU	NORTH DUBLIN UNION
NCO	NON-COMMISSIONED OFFICER
OC	OFFICER COMMANDING
O/O	OPERATIONS ORDER
OP	OBSERVATION POST
QMG	QUARTER MASTER GENERAL
RAF	ROYAL AIR FORCE
RAMC	ROYAL ARMY MEDICAL CORPS
RAOC	ROYAL ARMY ORDNANCE CORPS
RA.SC	ROYAL ARMY SUPPLY CORPS
RAVC	ROYAL ARMY VETERINARY CORPS
RE	ROYAL ENGINEERS
RFA	ROYAL FIELD ARTILLERY
RGA	ROYAL GARRISON ARTILLERY
RIC	ROYAL IRISH CONSTABULARY
ROIR	RESTORATION OF ORDER IN IRELAND REGULATIONS
RTO	RAILWAY TRANSPORT OFFICER
SAA	SMALL ARMS AMMUNITION
SR	SPECIAL RESERVE
S & T	SUPPLY AND TRANSPORT
TF	TERRITORIAL FORCE

Preface

DURING MY RESEARCH over the past few years, I have been able to explore much of the British primary material of the War of Independence. In *British Voices*, I edited the accounts of British servicemen who served in Ireland. This second book contains key documents of the Irish War of Independence the main one being the 'Dublin District Historical Record'. This work is part of the official British history of the war in Ireland, known as 'Record of the Rebellion in Ireland, 1920-1921 (Vol. IV, Part III)' which is now preserved in the National Archives in Kew. To this has been added an extract from the intelligence history specific to the Dublin campaign from Vol. II, Record of the Rebellion (Intelligence), and brief biographies of the key British commanders in Dublin and some biographies of the British officers killed on 21 November 1920 have been included.

I would like to thank the always professional and courteous staff of the National Archives, who have been a great assistance to me over the last few years, and the National Archives for their permission to reproduce these documents. Finally I would like to thank Dr Maura Cronin, my supervisor, who has been an invaluable help to me over the past few years.

This is the second of three edited books of primary sources of the British campaign in Ireland which will make this material available to both historians and interested members of the public and will, I hope, be of assistance in balancing the popular understanding of the campaign.

The documents have been reproduced as accurately as possible from the originals. Some changes in presentation have been necessary due to publishing requirements, and dates have been changed to the publisher's house style.

WILLIAM SHEEHAN
EDITOR
March 2007

Editor's Introduction

FOLLOWING ALMOST ALL significant conflicts in which the British army was engaged, an official history of the campaign was written and published. This was partly to commemorate the war in question and partly to capture and disseminate the lessons learned. Ireland's War of Independence was no exception. However, in this case, this history, the 'Record of the Rebellion in Ireland' was not published and rests in the files of the National Archives.

Two sections of this are reproduced here. The core of this book is a reproduction of the 'Dublin District Historical Record' contained in Vol. IV of the Record of the Rebellion. Appendix A contains the elements of Vol. II (Intelligence) which deal with intelligence matters in Dublin. They are reproduced here together for the first time for a general readership. The main section detailing the operations of the Dublin District retains the feeling of a first draft, and lacks detail in many areas. It is, however, still of great value to the historian or interested reader. One of the original reasons behind the commissioning of this history by the general staff was that it was also intended to provide instruction in the area of partisan warfare, and the reader will find this coming through in certain sections which provide instructions and suggestions for future campaigns. In many ways it is a very practical military document.

This was the first serious urban insurgency the British army was to face. As the years advanced, they would face the same challenges again in Jerusalem, Nicosia, Kuala Lumpur and Nairobi. The appendices contained in the documents detail the standing orders of the British commanders in Dublin, and their solutions to some of the tactical difficulties faced. Some of the areas addressed include: patrolling in an urban environment, the conduct of cordon and search operations, the protection of road and rail convoys, and the employment of armoured cars. It would be interesting to look for comparison at standing orders in the most recent conflicts in Iraq and Afghanistan.

In the Irish imagination, the War of Independence is remembered primarily as a war of flying columns, a rural campaign in isolated hills and mountains. However, the urban insurgency in Dublin was a key focus of the British army. This was a twentieth-century conflict, and one of the most interesting aspects of the official history is its treatment of the use of technology by the British army in Dublin. One of the many areas examined by the history, and which will be unfamiliar to many interested in the war, is the employment of aircraft in support of Dublin District operations. Aeroplanes were used to disperse crowds near Mountjoy, distribute propaganda leaflets by air, and provide armed protection to convoys and trains. The 'Dublin District Historical Record' also shows that towards the end, aerial reconnaissance was becoming important for the army, leading to the finding of arms dumps in the Wicklow Mountains, and for the monitoring of the IRA during the

Truce. Wireless radio was distributed to most units before the Truce, and the process completed afterwards, being considered vital in securing military communications from IRA interception. Armoured cars were routinely deployed on operations in Dublin, to provide greater protection to soldiers, conserve manpower and strengthen offensive operations, while searchlights were critical to the enforcement of the curfew. But one of the most intriguing images conjured by the history is the picture of an officer of the Royal Engineers sitting in the cellars of Dublin Castle, using a listening set to detect potential IRA mining operations.

One of the enduring popular beliefs about the war is that the British army failed to cope with the IRA an idea continues that they could not adapt to the circumstances in Ireland. However, one thing that will strike the reader from the 'Dublin District Historical Record' is the capacity to learn shown by the army in Dublin. Urban patrolling was refined as the campaign progressed. Stop and search methods were also improved. Specialist units were developed, such as an auxiliary unit for ship searches. Population control was imposed and refined, particularly the application of curfew hours, and restrictions were even applied to the use of bicycles. The creation of flying columns by the IRA was actually welcomed by the British army, as it finally gave them a clear target for offensive operations.

One of the most powerful sentiments running through the 'Dublin District Historical Record' is the criticism of the politicians, particularly of their lack of action, support and understanding for the army's problems in Ireland. The history firmly attributes the responsibility for the army's greatest difficulties in Dublin to ill-judged government decisions, not to the actions of the IRA. A key belief is that the government lacked a consistent and understandable policy, resulting in a failure to deliver key resources like manpower and equipment. The army believed that many of the decisions taken by the Cabinet actually strengthened the IRA's position. The government's release of hunger strikers is in particular singled out as reviving a nearly finished IRA, and renewing the IRA faith in its campaign. It notes from a practical view that the released IRA could then target the police officers and informers who imprisoned them. One is left to wonder if the overt attacks on the political management of the war would have been edited out of the final draft.

The death of British officers on 21 November 1920 is seen from a different perspective by the writers of the 'Dublin District Historical Record'. It is not seen as the body blow to British Intelligence in Dublin, as often portrayed in nationalist history. Instead, it is considered as an attempt to disrupt the administrative work of the general headquarters, rather than an attempt to destroy the intelligence system. Indeed, when one examines the nature of the posts held by some of the officers killed, one can begin to understand this point of view. Two of the officers killed, Captain Newberry and Captain Baggallery, were both court-martials officers, and Lt-Col Montgomery's background would indicate he was a staff officer. The others who died, Major Dowling, Captain Price, Lieutenants Maclean, Ames, Angliss, Murray, Bennett, and Cadets Morris and Garniss were all undoubtedly engaged in Intelligence work. One of the interesting points raised by the personnel files which are held in the National Archives at Kew is the question of nationality; Ames was an American, and Angliss was Irish. Instructions in their personnel files were clear that their names not be printed in the army lists, and they were not paid through regular channels. They were, in fact, paid through the army agents, Cox and Co, in Charing Cross in London, to whom they had to submit monthly expenses, a case of out of the army but not escaped from its bureaucracy. These instructions were absent for the files of Montgomery and Newberry. However, none of these men were in Dublin very long. Most had only been in the city a month or two, which meant that they can have had little time to develop contacts or a detailed familiarity with the situation in the city. Ironically, though those killed were remembered as the 'Cairo gang', the remaining service records do not show any service in the Middle East. The loss to the British forces was in personnel and potential rather than in existing key intelligence officers. The official history reports, 'Sinn Féin had in no way impeded the activities of the military by this outrage'. In the opinion of the authors of the 'Dublin District Historical Record', far more damaging to their cause was a decision by GHQ and the police to transfer Dublin District Intelligence to police control, a move they believed damaged military operations for months. However, the intelligence history takes a different view.

Sinn Féin was identified as being closely linked with socialism and trade unionism. Indeed, for many British observers of the Irish situation of the time, Sinn Féin was seen as a form of 'green Bolshevism'.

Given the rise of the Soviet Union during this period, and labour difficulties in England, it is perhaps an understandable error. In the end, it is interesting to reflect that the group which the British army considered as causing the majority of their difficulties in Dublin was British politicians. There is, in this document, a sense of satisfaction, of a war well fought in testing circumstances, a sense that only the Truce prevented the destruction of the IRA. In the end, the army felt it was Cabinet robbed them of their victory, not the IRA.

Dublin District Historical Record

CHAPTER I

Summary of Events in Dublin during 1919

Political Situation

The situation began to assume a serious aspect in Dublin early in 1919, when various political meetings were held in the city in furtherance of the Irish republican movement, and the actions of government and police were denounced in correction with the arrest and treatment of political prisoners.

First Attack on DMP (June)

As a result of these violent speeches, the first attack was made on DMP in Dublin in June, 1919, following the suppression of a political meeting in the Mansion House; fire was opened on the police in Dawson Street and four officers were wounded.

Towards the end of July 1919, a detective sergeant, who was engaged on political duty, while returning to his home at night, was fired on by a number of armed men and mortally wounded.

During this year the police made numerous searches of residences of political suspects for arms, ammunition, etc. Following a search of Sinn Féin headquarters (6 Harcourt Street) in September, when two prominent suspects who were wanted were arrested, a detective officer of the DMP was shot dead in Gt. Brunswick Street when returning from the raid. After this murder feeling became very hostile towards the police, and on 19 October, 1919, a constable was shot in High Street; 29 November 1919, a detective sergeant was shot in College Street. The attempted murder of two other detective officers, one of whom was seriously wounded, took place about the same time.

Attack on HE The Viceroy (December)
On 19 December a well organised attempt was made on the life of His Excellency Lord French at Ashtown, when one of the attackers was shot dead, and two DMP were wounded.

Destruction of Independent Newspaper Plant (December)
Owing to the condemnation of this outrage expressed by the *Independent* newspaper, the premises were raided by about 40 armed men who destroyed the whole plant, damage estimated at about £40,000.

Dáil Éireann, etc., Proclaimed
About November, 1919, Dáil Éireann, Sinn Féin, Cumann na mBan, the Gaelic League and kindred organisations were suppressed by the order of government, also a number of seditious newspapers.

Murder of Mr. Redmond, Assistant Commissioner, DMP
In January, 1920, the assistant commissioner of the Dublin Metropolitan Police, while proceeding to his residence in Harcourt Street, was shot dead by a number of armed men.

CHAPTER II

Period: January 1920 to May 1920 (Inclusive)

Dublin District HQ and Area

The Dublin District Headquarters formed on a divisional basis, under Major-General G.F. Boyd, CB, CMG, DSO, DCM, came into existence and replaced the 13th Infantry Brigade Headquarters on 1 January 1920 (*see* Appendix XIII.)

Although the new staff was in excess of the previous Brigade staff it was insufficient. The command included 17 units, of which nine were Infantry battalions, one Cavalry regiment, and a Machine Gun battalion (*see* Appendix I). There were no Brigade Headquarters at this stage. The general staff of one second, one third grade GSO, and an attached officer for Intelligence, could not cope efficiently with such an unwieldy formation. Application was therefore made for two Brigade Headquarter staffs.

24th and 25th (P.) Brigades

The two Brigade Headquarters were finally sanctioned and came into being on 19 April 1920, as the 24th and 25th Provisional Brigades. (For the brigade areas *see* Appendix XIII, and for composition, Appendix I.)

Political Situation and Condition of the DMP

Meanwhile the political situation in Dublin city was serious, the murder of police continued. The DMP 'G' (detective) Division had been virtually driven off the streets, and the remainder of the force was of little value as regards crime with a political object. Thus additional onus for maintaining order was thrown on the troops and the GOC, Dublin District (except for administrative duties) became virtually head of the police in the city. In January, at the request of the Chief Commissioner, DMP, occasional patrolling of the city by the troops in support of the DMP commenced.

Raids by Troops

The first actual raids by troops were carried out about middle of January, resulting in several important arrests. But the lack of information, in spite of the individual efforts of a few officers to obtain it, made success very difficult. It was obvious that an organised Intelligence system was essential, and with this end in view, application was made for a Special Intelligence officer to be appointed to Dublin District Headquarters.

First formation of Intelligence System

This officer ultimately arrived in February, and at once commenced to organise and expand the few Intelligence facilities that existed. The personnel at his disposal consisted of a few officers due for demobilisation, the remnants of 'G' Division, DMP, and a few plain clothes RIC. Small sums of money, borrowed from the Chief Commissioner, DMP, were available for Secret Service work. The organising of the Dublin District Intelligence immediately bore fruit.

Information became available and gave objectives for raids.

Cullenswood House HQ IRA, M. Collins (February)

Military raids for important Sinn Féiners became more numerous; the information gained from raids led to further captures, culminating in the discovery of the IRA Headquarters at Cullenswood House in February, where complete rolls and addresses of 3,000 members of the Dublin IRA Brigade were found. By March, the majority of the local Sinn Féin and IRA leaders had been arrested and confined in Mountjoy Prison.

First Curfew

On 23 February the first curfew restriction was put into force in Dublin, no civilian being permitted to be outside his dwelling between the hours of midnight and 5am in the Dublin Metropolitan area, less 'F' Division (Kingstown area). The curfew restrictions were generally obeyed from the outset, and little trouble was experienced. Initially some twenty military patrols (each of one officer and twelve other ranks) in motor lorries or on cycles patrolled the city. These were gradually reduced and it was found that two or three patrols nightly were sufficient.

(March) Satisfactory Situation

Although the military activity had increased, nevertheless the rebels continued to confine their attacks to the police. But matters in Dublin were now looking black for Sinn Féin, many leaders were in our hands, and the activity of the Crown forces was on the increase.

Hunger Strike

It was therefore decided to employ new methods against us, chiefly as a form of propaganda; and a hunger strike by political prisoners commenced in Mountjoy Prison on 5 April 1920. Much of this was bluff, but great propaganda was made of the affair by the Irish, and part of the British press. A so-called sympathetic strike on the part of the transport workers was called on 11 April, as a protest against the retention of the hunger strikers.

Trouble at Mountjoy Prison

Meanwhile on the 12 and 13 [April] large and menacing crowds (in some cases up to 20,000) congregated around Mountjoy. Additional troops were required to guard the Prison, the warders' houses, the local DMP barracks, and to keep the roads clear. But the approaches to Mountjoy became blocked with people. Communication by telephone with the officer in charge of the troops remained available.

Use of Aeroplanes

The futility of committing troops to hold back such a crowd (including many women) was soon obvious. Rapidly constructed obstacles were soon trodden down by the leading ranks of the crowd being pressed forward from behind; even tanks were no obstacle. The troops thus found themselves in the unenviable position of being either overwhelmed or having to open fire on a somewhat passive, but advancing crowd of men and women. Fortunately the crowd was persuaded to desist from pressing further on the troops, and it finally dispersed. But matters looked very black at one time, and it seemed that bloodshed could not be avoided. Intrepid work was done by the Air Force on the 13th with low-flying planes, in spite of a 50-mile gale of wind, and the proximity of the houses. In one case an aeroplane flew along a broad street below the eaves of the houses. This clearly demonstrated that aeroplanes could be used for clearing streets by dropping warning notices and if necessary, using Lewis gunfire.

Release of Hunger Strikers

On the 14th the DMP were withdrawn from their local barracks, which enabled the military dispositions at Mountjoy to be altered. Troops were posted inside or on the prison walls and buildings. In this position comparatively few troops were sufficient to guard the prison. On this date the British government decided to release the political prisoners who were on hunger strike.

Military Summary

At this stage battalions in Dublin were strong but the majority of men were inexperienced. Since the beginning of the year it had become more obvious that military control in Dublin City was necessary for the maintenance of law and order. Under DORA, which was in force at this time, the powers of the military commander were considerable, and by the month of March full use of them became necessary.

The organisation of the military resources had therefore to be made rather with a view to policing than military operations. Numerous patrols and raiding parties became necessary in the city, tasks of comparatively short duration, but frequently extended areas had to be covered. The need for motor transport and cycles for tactical (patrol, etc.) work therefore became urgent. Each battalion in Dublin was allotted one 3-ton lorry for tactical work and at least 30 cycles. In spite of its slowness and noise the 3-ton lorry proved invaluable in the city, especially during this period (January–April, 1920). The supply of good drivers was always a problem.

One of the greatest difficulties initially was the question of communications. The military telephones were largely controlled by the GPO, which was impregnated with Sinn Féin. A few direct lines did exist, but the danger of having our lines tapped or interrupted was obvious. Application was therefore made for wireless installations and for immediate use 'maroon signals' as the 'S.O.S.' signal were demanded for each group of barracks.

The only other military operation of note, not already included, that took place during March was the establishment of a blockade line across Ireland in conjunction with the 5th Division. In Dublin District the line of the river Liffey west of Dublin and the Northern canal in the city was taken. All roads crossing the line were watched by piquets, with the object of preventing an extensive movement of IRA from the south to Ulster. The precautions were successful in that no such movement took place.

CHAPTER III

Period: May 1920 to December 1920

Results of the Release of the Hunger Strikers
The release of the hunger strikers by the Government was looked on as a great victory for Sinn Féin. Certainly, results derogatory to us were soon apparent. The Military and Police Secret Services personnel were virtually driven off the streets, owing to those whom they had arrested now being free, and in many cases able to identify our agents. This necessitated a temporary cessation of our secret service activities.

The curfew restrictions remained in force but otherwise the military and police activities abated, partly by order and partly through lack of information. The IRA soon realised these changes, and its moral and truculence began to increase accordingly.

Troops Training
The month of May was passed by the troops in carrying out musketry and training. Many of the men had scarcely fired a rifle, and the majority had never been exercised on a classification range.

Re-organisation of Intelligence (May)

Dublin District Headquarters Intelligence was again re-organised. A first grade Staff officer for Intelligence had been appointed, who commenced work in May. Authority had been given to employ demobilised officers on Intelligence work. The whole system was, therefore, reorganised and expanded (*see* Intelligence, Dublin District Rebellion, 1919-1921 [Appendix A, this book]). The lull in our activities was employed in initiating the new Secret Service personnel into Dublin.

Co-operation between Military and Police

The defence of military and police barracks was re-considered, with a view to co-operation, and the release of a maximum for offensive duties. The system of numerous isolated RIC barracks in the country was a constant source of anxiety. In many cases the number of police in a RIC detachment was so small that they were practically confined to their own immediate neighbourhood by day, and to their barracks by night. Such conditions were obviously bad for the moral of the police, and good for that of the IRA.

Military Detachments (June)

Military detachments were therefore placed in Counties Meath, Dublin, and Wicklow, at central points, and as far as possible in the immediate proximity of the RIC, who consented to concentrate on their most important barracks. Each military detachment was finally supplied with at least two motor vehicles, to be used as a small tactical column for offensive duties. The reduction of outlying and weak RIC barracks enabled these military detachments at a later date to devote their activities to hunting rebels, instead of having to adopt a defensive role in trying to keep touch with numerous ineffective police detachments. The RIC were available to act as guides and furnish the troops with information.

Communications

The question of keeping touch with the various military and police detachments was difficult. In some cases rocket signals were sufficient to pass the alarm locally, but nothing short of wireless between every military detachment was reliable. The installation of wireless to this extent was ultimately completed in August, 1921. The time required to train personnel was the cause of the delay, as no trained Wireless operators were available, and the personnel had to be taken and trained from the Infantry.

From its commencement, each military detachment constructed a dropping circle, for receiving messages by aeroplane. Later, a special identification sign at each dropping circle was found necessary, as the rebels were apt to construct bogus ones.

Meanwhile, in Dublin, similar arrangements were made to affiliate the DMP barracks to the nearest unit, and a system of signals was arranged.

Although the decentralisation of responsibility for keeping touch with the police was an improvement, it was found that the only satisfactory method of solving the whole question of co-operation between the military and the police was to make the local Military Commander responsible for the actual safety of definite police barracks. In the country districts each Detachment Commander was finally (in July) made responsible for law and order in a definite area. The detachment areas were described as circles, and allotted on the ratio of half a Company Infantry up to an area of between 5 and 10 miles radius, each military detachment being ultimately complete with at least two MT vehicles. Initially, the shortage of MT and drivers seriously hampered the scheme.

Situation in May

In Dublin District, towards the end of May, the murder campaign by the rebels against the police and attacks on their barracks re-opened. The IRA had been reorganised, and the formation of the women's legion (Cumn na mBan [sic]) had been pushed forward.

Dockers' Strike (June)

Meanwhile, the extreme labour element and Sinn Féin had drawn more together, and finally, in June, the dock labourers at North Wall, Dublin, came into the open by refusing to handle munitions for the Crown forces. The reply to this action was a lock-out by the LNW Railway Co., who at once called for, and obtained, military protection.

Demands on Dublin Garrison

Government stores, such as arms, munitions, clothing, motor transport, etc., had now to be transported in Government ships and handled by military labour. Special provision also became necessary for the protection of petrol, and the large Shell Trading Company reserves at North Wall were guarded and stocks in the country were seized for safe custody. This work became very heavy on the troops in Dublin, which virtually became the base for the majority of the Crown forces in

Ireland. The quays where such stores were landed had to be specially guarded. The question of guards was a continual source of worry and loss of initiative to the troops in Dublin. The garrison guards throughout hostilities (apart from barrack guards) averaged daily some 400 officers and other ranks. This was obviously a serious drain to the offensive power of the military garrison. In some cases adequate guards were not available, and through political pressure it was necessary to post guards that could serve no useful military purpose.

'King's Inn' (June)

The first military reverse in Dublin was the surprise of one of these guards in June, at the 'King's Inn' a Government legal records office. The guard, consisting of a NCO and twelve other ranks, although isolated, as far as possible, from the public, who were at liberty to use the buildings, was finally surprised and lost its arms. The only advantage of this reverse was to make the Government realise the futility of posting innumerable guards ineffective through weakness, and three guards were withdrawn. One of these being that at the Custom House, which otherwise would probably have been burnt out with the buildings when they were destroyed in June, 1921.

(June) *Sinn Féin Policy*

Sinn Féin activities were now directed in a new direction. Great efforts were made to usurp the functions of the Local Government Board by controlling the County Councils and Tax collectors. Together with this movement, land grabbing commenced, which ultimately proved more of an embarrassment to Sinn Féin than a help.

Curfew

On 30 June, curfew in Dublin was relaxed to the hours midnight to 3am, according to the daylight. In Dublin city more hostility was shown to soldiers, and cases of firing at sentries were reported. Information was also received that officers and men would probably be molested in the streets. Orders were therefore issued in May warning all ranks to keep to main thoroughfares and be vigilant. The issue of automatic pistols had been sanctioned.

Military Activities Reopen

Military patrols were again sent out into the streets to support the DMP. In order to make sufficient troops available for these duties it was necessary to slow down the musketry and withdraw troops from Kilbride (Musketry Camp).

RIC Boycott (July)

In early July efforts to boycott the RIC were first experienced in Co. Wicklow. This never proved an effective weapon, as the police took by force and payed for what they required.

Sinn Féin Police and Policy

A new force known as the Sinn Féin Police was now formed. In some parts of Co. Meath these police became active, especially where no Crown forces were in the vicinity. The normal hours for opening and closing public houses were altered by Sinn Féin, but not generally enforced. In fact, much of their spasmodic effort at local government was for propaganda abroad.

Further endeavours were made to embroil the Crown

forces with Irish labour, and thereby with British labour. In many cases it was difficult to differentiate between a labour and Sinn Féin meeting, the former being used frequently as a cloak for the latter.

Military Activity (July)
The Military Intelligence had now become active again, with the result that raids by troops for Sinn Féin leaders, and dumps of arms, munitions, etc., recommenced. The first mobile column was used about this time in Dublin District, a mixed force of squadron of Cavalry and company of Infantry being sent from Dublin vicinity to round up a race meeting at Bellewstown (Co. Meath), 20 miles distant, which was being policed by Sinn Féin Police. The operation proved to be simple, the troops effected a rendezvous in the proximity undetected, the Infantry arriving by motor transport. The Sinn Féin Police were surrounded without resistance and made to look foolish.

Railways closed to Military Stores and Crown forces (July)
Following on the dockers' strike in June, every obstruction was offered to the Crown forces by the railway employees throughout the country (except on the Great Northern line) until, owing to the activity on the part of the railway employees against the military services, large numbers of the former were dismissed. The railway services throughout the country were thus becoming reduced. This had been foreseen by the military authorities, who commenced in August to transport their stores by motor transport in Dublin District and other parts of the country except in the case of the Great

Northern Railway. Although military protection for the Great Northern Railway was considered, none was found necessary except the guarding of the Drogheda railway bridge. The Sinn Féin reply to our use of motor transport was to cut the roads (later).

Meanwhile, parties of the Crown forces continued to board the trains, the immediate result being the refusal of the guards and drivers to function. The railway company were then compelled to dismiss these employees, and the working of the railways became more and more chaotic. This affected the convenience of the civil population, and caused widespread unemployment of railway employees through dismissal, the onus falling on Sinn Féin.

Political Situation (August)

Sinn Féin was exerting every means of spreading their propaganda, especially in the United States of America. Great display was made of the attitude adopted by the Lord Mayor of Cork (hunger strike). Efforts were also made about this time to suppress the sale of English journals unfavourable to Sinn Féin.

Although the attitude of the elder clergy was now clearly against the extremist element, the younger members of the Church were active supporters of it. In this dilemma, the Church offered little restraining influence.

The situation in Dublin city was meanwhile getting worse. The Communist Labour Party had thrown in their lot with Sinn Féin. Threats of a general rising in the event of the Lord Mayor of Cork being allowed to die were uttered. Meanwhile, rebel activity against military and police patrols commenced, chiefly in the form of sniping.

Armouring of Lorries

The work of armouring 3-ton lorries had commenced, which proved very satisfactory for work in the city, providing there was head cover sufficient to prevent bombs falling into the lorry. The drivers of tactical vehicles were provided with body armour.

Military Activities, ROIR (August)

The military situation in Dublin had, on the other hand, improved. On 13 August the Restoration of Order in Ireland Act came into force, giving the competent military authorities great powers. The 24th and 25th Brigade Commanders became competent military authorities. The Intelligence Service was working effectively again. Much information became available, and the number of military raids increased. These were directed against leaders, active members and dumps.

Air Mail

In August, owing to the danger of civil facilities, the military air mail service was commenced between Baldonnell aerodrome and the formations in the country.

Collection of Arms (August)

In September the rebels made a new move, evidently owing to shortage of arms and ammunition. This was a general raid of civilians who were known to, or likely to, possess firearms of any description. Generally speaking, no opposition was offered to these raids. It was therefore decided by the military authorities to call in all arms from civilians, the issue of permits for arms having been in the hands of the competent military authority since July. This proved to be an effective but laborious business.

Some 40,000 shot guns alone were ultimately collected into Island Bridge ordnance depot. All arms were surrendered to the nearest military or police post, and forwarded thence to Ordnance. Special arrangements had to be made for labelling and periodical overhaul of these weapons.

Rebels 'On the Run' (September)

It now became evident that our raiding activity was bearing other fruit than captures. Large numbers of rebels were permanently on the run, many sleeping in the hedgerows and hayricks. Frequent changes of quarters were made. This was good news, especially with the winter approaching.

Military 'Hold-ups'

For several weeks systematic hold-ups at irregular times by military and police had taken place throughout the city and district. The main object was to interfere with the rebel communications and check motor permits. It was known that motor cars, cycles, ordinary cycles and later, railway guards and drivers, were used for carrying dispatches. Although we were not successful in achieving any definite capture of despatches by these methods, it was discovered that our activity considerably hampered their arrangements.

Use of Aeroplanes

Periodical reconnaissance by aeroplanes over suspected and suitable areas was now instituted. Suitable opportunities were especially offered by the openness of the terrain in the Wicklow Hills. This area was also known to be used by the rebels for training and dumps. Useful results were achieved so long as the weather remained favourable for flying. The aeroplane inspired a fearsome dread in the rebels, who at first showed little knowledge of hiding themselves. The great handicap to the Air Force in Ireland was that no arms were permitted to be carried in the aeroplanes. On one occasion an aeroplane pursued rebels who had seized a RAF motor car. Owing to the alertness of the pilot the car was overhauled in a very short time, but nothing could be done, as the pilot and observer were unarmed.

Ambush and Arrest of Kevin Barry

At the end of September a regrettable incident occurred in Dublin City. A small military escort (1 and 6, 2nd Bn. Duke of Wellington's Regiment), whilst drawing bread, was surprised, and three young soldiers were killed. The remainder, however, drove off the attackers and captured one of them (the notorious Kevin Barry, found hiding under the lorry).

Trim Police Barracks

On 26 September the RIC police barracks at Trim were captured through treachery, and destroyed by rebels. This is the only case of occupied police barracks in the Dublin District being captured.

Decrease of IRA Moral (October)

The pressure of the Crown forces had become so severe by the beginning of October that the rebels were compelled to adopt some new expedient. The British Government remained firm as regards the Lord Mayor of Cork. This attitude undoubtedly had a strong effect, and in some degree awakened slight confidence amongst the Loyalists.

Sinn Féin Police (October)

Sinn Féin gave up for the time its civil activities and concentrated on the military work. Every endeavour was made
to spread the IRA organisation and re-establish its moral.
But little headway was made in the Dublin District area. The
Fingal Brigade in North Co. Dublin had become active again,
but in October it was completely broken up by the round up
of Swords, and the remnants went 'on the run'.

Fernside, Drumcondra

On 12 October Fernside, Drumcondra, was raided by a few
Intelligence officers. Unfortunately two officers were killed
(Major Smythe, DSO, and Captain White), but at least two
rebels lost their lives, and the notorious Dan Breen was
badly wounded.

Death of Lord Mayor of Cork

During the third week of October the Lord Mayor of Cork
died. The firmness of the British Government in his case had
a far-reaching effect in reviving confidence. In Dublin a further deterioration of the IRA moral was noticeable. For the
first time ammunition was found abandoned by the rebels,
whilst considerable captures of rebel arsenals were effected
by the troops in Dublin, notably at Eustace Street.

Talbot Street

On 14 November, on receipt of information that a
Republican meeting was in progress at the Republican Stores,

Talbot Street (Dublin), one officer, twenty other ranks (1st Lancashire Fusiliers), with an armoured car, were sent at once from the Castle to raid the place. On arrival the alarm was given and it has since been ascertained that one of the rebels deliberately exposed himself in the street, opening fire to divert our attention. Fire was also opened from the house. This man (Treacy) was killed, and also several other civilians. Of the Crown forces, one was killed and three wounded. The Stores were searched, but by this time the meeting had broken up. All the IRA leaders had been present.

Motor Permit Order

On 14 November a proclamation by the competent military authority, GHQ, was issued restricting from 1 December the use of motor vehicles and motor cycles without a permit and beyond a radius of 20 miles from the garage without special permit (sparingly granted, and only for definite journeys).

Murders, 21 November

Finally the rebels' desperation culminated in the murder of eight officers, two auxiliaries, and the wounding of four officers (two mortally) on 21 November (*see* Appendix II). The object of this outrage was probably to smash the machinery of Dublin District Headquarters. The addresses of the General Staff and QMG Staff officers who lived out, were all visited, and also those of known Courts Martial and Intelligence officers. Fortunately in many cases the officers wanted were no longer living out and in one case the officer escaped. At some addresses where a number of officers and their wives lived together, the murderers became confused and took lives that were not intended.

The question of officers and other ranks living out and being armed had naturally arisen before 21 November. The same had arisen as regards the men walking out. Although rumours had been received to the effect, it was never seriously believed that officers other than those connected with Intelligence or murder trials, were in serious danger of their lives. The officers primarily affected under the above headings had been brought in, previous to 21 November. The damage of such an outrage to the rebel cause had been looked on as the chief factor against its taking place. Mulcahy in his letter captured about 19 November foreshadowed the shooting of animals, and outrages in England, and interference with the movements of officers. The decision against any change was come to on these considerations, together with the bad moral effect of prematurely bringing the officers into barracks, and the expense to individuals of such a move. The question of carrying arms had also been fully considered. An officer living isolated from assistance, if known to possess a weapon, would have been an object of raiding. Where it appeared that officers retaining their arms had a good chance of being able to make good use of them they were encouraged to do so. Orders were therefore issued in July 1920 that it was not intended for officers always to carry arms, but that they should be in possession of an efficient weapon and be capable of making good use of it.

Croke Park, 21 November
Information was received that a meeting of the IRA would be held under the cover of the Croke Park football match on

the afternoon, 21 November. It was decided to surround the whole enclosure and search the people as they were passed out. A mixed force of infantry, armoured cars, Auxiliaries and RIC was employed, under the command of the 24th Brigade Commander. The RIC contingent arrived prematurely and report that on entering the ground they were fired on. The police returned the fire, killing fourteen civilians. Before the cordon of troops could be completed a stampede by the crowd had taken place and no arrests were made.

Great Military Activity

As a result of the 21 November outrage, intense activity by the Crown forces commenced throughout Dublin District. A general round-up of the Dublin IRA brigade was commenced, at the rate of about one hundred raids each twenty-four hours. It was hoped by these means to arrest many who had taken part in the Sunday murders. Undoubtedly this was successful, but identification was difficult. Meanwhile, the rebel activity ceased completely. Never had Dublin been so quiet. The feeling of the public throughout the district was generally against the Sunday murders. Sinn Féin had in no way impeded the activities of the military by this outrage, and its own affairs were now at a low ebb. The Irish Press favourable to Sinn Féin had become frightened.

In Dublin the troops were unlucky not to capture Richard Mulcahy, Chief of Staff, IRA; he managed to escape in his night attire but his office fell into our hands.

Curfew

On Monday, 22 November, Arthur Griffiths was taken into

custody, chiefly for his own safety, and curfew restrictions were extended in DMP area to the hours 10pm–5am. The railway strike was now beginning to show signs of failing, which ultimately occurred at a later date.

Action by Sinn Féin
Efforts were now made by Sinn Féin to carry out outrages in England. Burnings commenced in many parts of that country. In Ireland there was a movement to increase the Fianna (Boy Scouts) organisation and even furnish them with arms.

Flying Columns
Owing to the number of rebels 'on the run', these were formed into flying columns and made their first appearance in the south about this time (November).

Military Precautions
After the Sunday murders, the danger to officers and other ranks continuing to live out in Ireland became apparent. The War Office finally approved of special allowances to assist those who had to move and live apart from their families.

Officers to live in
Orders were issued by the Dublin District Headquarters that all officers must live within the protection of a military barracks and close to their work. Special quarters initially, including three hotels, had to be commandeered to effect this order. Officers were instructed to carry arms at all times and to go out in at least twos and threes. The men were ordered to go about in parties when on pass, and to use main streets.

Rebel ambushes in Dublin increase

The month of December was one of great activity in Dublin. The intensive raiding continued. Much information was obtained by these means and important captures were made. The rebels also endeavoured to increase their activity, chiefly by ambushing motor lorries and cars in Dublin. By this time many 3-ton lorries had been armoured and completed with overhead cover, but not in every case.

Few casualties were suffered by us and the troops soon became very alert and quick to take action. But it was always difficult to distinguish the rebels from the ordinary civilians in an ambush and many civilian casualties were caused by these outrages in Dublin. The rebel intention was to drive the military MT off the streets. But in this he absolutely failed and in his endeavours reduced his own moral.

Rebels use British Uniforms

During December cases were reported of the rebels using British and police uniforms. To guard against this danger, stringent orders were issued against permitting individuals or parties into any military barracks without proper identification.

Collapse of Railway Strike

On the 17 December the railway strike collapsed and the railways became available for military use, saving much MT and escort work.

Raid of Monasteries

Owing to evidence being captured pointing to the extensive use of monasteries by the IRA, it was found necessary to raid several. At least one Field officer was always present at these raids. On the whole, very little was ever discovered in a monastery or a church.

Military Summary
Defensive Measures

In May a special order was issued reminding all concerned of the necessity for maintaining thorough vigilance. The need for adequate defence arrangements and schemes in every barracks and guard was also emphasised. Sentries were to be covered by obstacles, especially in public places. The advantage and economy of sentry posts being selected in unapproachable and commanding positions became obvious. The orders for sentries in Dublin District were made clear as regards firing, namely:-

'A sentry will challenge twice, and then if he considers his post in danger and safety cannot be assured otherwise, will fire in order to hit the suspected person, and not at random. No more rounds will be expended than absolutely necessary.'

The principle of completing defences so that a maximum of the garrison might be available for offensive work was impressed on all.

Movement

The movement of small armed parties by march route through the streets of Dublin became dangerous. Instructions were therefore issued that parties of less than one officer and twenty other ranks would move through the city by motor transport. The danger of overcrowding vehicles had to be guarded against, and every man must know his task in the event of attack. Finally, in August, detailed orders were drawn up for armed parties moving by motor transport (*see* Appendix III).

Searchlights

In May the first Mobile Searchlights Section became available in Dublin District. This consisted of three lorries, each carrying one 60cm searchlight, and manned by experts (RE). The lights were used regularly in conjunction with curfew patrols. The usual method of use was to open the beam suddenly so as to surprise transgressors, but the light could not be used whilst the searchlight lorry was in motion.

The lights were also used in conjunction with raids but lights portable by hand were required for this work. The officer in charge of the section, therefore, with great ingenuity, arranged on one lorry five leads (up to 60 yards length each) with portable lights. These proved invaluable for raiding work. (For further use of Searchlight, *see* Military Summary of Chapter IV.)

Armoured Cars

Up to December there were two Rolls Royce (old, but effective), four Austin, and a few Jeffrey Quad armoured cars. The last named were never of much use, and spares were unobtainable. The Austin cars did excellent work, but by the end of the year 1920 they had all to be scrapped owing to the lack of spare parts. By this time, however, a new type of heavy armoured car had begun to appear, namely, the Peerless. They proved themselves to be excellent, especially in the streets of Dublin, where they were practically unstoppable. The total number of effective armoured cars in Dublin by the end of 1920 was two Rolls Royce and five Peerless. (For further expansion, *see* Chapter IV, Military Summary.)

The system of manning the cars was confusing, although it did work satisfactorily. The Rolls Royce cars were manned by and on the charge of the Armoured Car Company, the Peerless were driven by RASC drivers and the crews were drawn from the Infantry, the vehicles being on the charge of the RASC. As the number of cars increased, brigade sections of Peerless were formed by 24th and 25th Brigades, the Officer Commanding 5th Armoured Car Company acting as the general supervisor.

For city patrols and escort work the Peerless cars were invaluable and a great economy in manpower. In spite of the scratch crews, frequently working under a temporary lance-corporal (officers could not be spared), the results were excellent. With the exception of one regrettable incident when an armoured car was captured by the rebels, no untoward incident occurred. On the other hand it is fully acknowledged by the rebels that the moral effect of the cars was very considerable. The restraint displayed by the young Commanders and crews was most praiseworthy. Information was received from time to time that the rebels intended to mob and overturn an armoured car but this never occurred. (Standing Orders for Armoured Cars; *see* Appendix IV.)

Tanks
In August a number of old and various pattern tanks became

available for disposal, and permission was given to hand them over to the Infantry. Infantry crews were trained, and in the case of the more serviceable tanks most successful results were obtained. These so-called Infantry tanks were, however, generally used for defensive purposes in barracks, etc., and proved most useful.

One section of four male Mark V Star Tanks were available throughout 1920 and 1921. They were manned by Tank Corps personnel. Although never brought into action in Dublin, they would have been invaluable if required, their 6-pdr. armament affording an excellent protected and mobile artillery for warfare of this kind. On several occasions tanks were used in support to Infantry and armoured cars. The usual gate of walled barracks is too narrow for a tank to pass without the sponsons [gun platform] being taken in, which is a slow business. The majority of bridges in and about Dublin will not carry heavy tanks.

Communications

In addition to civil telephones and telegraphs, wireless, as explained above, was gradually being installed. As detachments became located in the country, a pigeon service was opened up, the loft being situated at Dublin District Headquarters in the Castle. Birds had to be changed at least twice a week and they were generally sent down through the railways. It is curious that this method of despatch was not interfered with appreciably by the rebels. Each detachment set up a dropping circle, and in the event of emergency, messages could have been sent to them by aeroplane. Certain light signal rockets had also to be arranged in conjunction with this service, as a means of drawing attention and reporting 'SOS'. The Popham

Panel [signalling system] was issued later to each detachment.

Clino Machines

In September an issue of clino-combination cycles [motorcycles] was made to several battalions, all units being ultimately completed to two machines. These machines were specially useful in the country, in conjunction with motor transport, cavalry or infantry, acting as scouts, or for reconnoitring and despatch riding purposes. The infantry supplied their own drivers, who were trained by the RASC. Each machine was capable of carrying a Lewis gun if required.

Stokes

Originally there was one battery of four mortars in the district, but this was expanded finally to two mortars per battalion. This weapon would have been invaluable if the occasion had arisen. They were regularly taken out when extensive operations were being carried out. Also used as a protection to important convoys, and for the defence of barracks. Stokes bombs were carried by motor transport in the country, for blowing up road blocks.

Mining

In Dublin City, where barracks, such as the Castle, are contiguous with civilian dwellings, the possibility of hostile mining is always present. In Dublin Castle extensive investigations were made with the view of detecting such work. A special RE officer, equipped with listening sets, was found to be essential. Later, as the rebels escaped from internment camps by means of tunnelling, the probability of mining operations became more probable.

Explosives for Quarries

To prevent avoidable unemployment it was essential to keep the quarries in the country supplied with explosives required for their work. This entailed much detailed arrangement, and was a heavy call on the troops for escort duty. In Dublin District the explosive was issued in limited amounts from the magazine on CMA authority. Thence it was escorted to its destination, where it was at once used during the presence of the escort.

Auxiliaries

In May, 'F' Company, Auxiliary Division, RIC, was placed at the disposal of Dublin District for operations. The Chief of Police continued to carry out the administration of the company, but otherwise the company came under the orders of the GOC, Dublin District. This company was quartered in the Castle, and used for urgent operations and raids, by direct order from the headquarters.

In November two additional companies ('I' and 'J') were also allocated to Dublin District by the Chief of Police. One was affiliated to each of the 24th and 25th Brigades. These companies were relieved from time to time by 'N', 'C', and 'R'. On the whole the work of the Auxiliaries in Dublin was excellent, and the happiest relations existed between them and the troops.

Raids

In October it became apparent that the rebels contemplated interfering with military raiding parties. Instructions were therefore issued that each battalion should detail daily a duty platoon (as far as possible) of an officer and twenty other ranks for sudden raids. These parties were to practise raids in barracks, taking into account the probable rebel action. It was pointed out that the IRA possessed weapons with at least 200 yards range. The importance of having light available by night during raids was also emphasised. Even the strong headlights of armoured cars were useful.

By early November many raids had been carried out, frequently with no obvious result. This was discouraging to the troops. It was therefore decided to point out the importance of what seemed at first sight futile raids. Our activities were causing large numbers of rebels to go 'on the run'. Support had to be obtained from the attenuated Sinn Féin funds.

At the same time the GOC marked his appreciation of the courtesy shown by the troops on raids. He emphasised the importance of such conduct as likely to establish confidence, in that innocent civilians began to realise that they had nothing to fear from a military raid.

Special instructions were also issued on the following subjects:
(a) Officers not to move about with important documents on them
(b) Safe custody of arms and ammunition
(c) Steel helmets useful in the town, but not so generally required in the country
(d) *Instruction for firing in the event of civil disturbance:-*

(i) A sentry will challenge at least twice before firing, and must then usually act on his own initiative.

(ii) Indiscriminate firing by troops is not permitted, and is thoroughly bad for moral and discipline. *Troops will fire by order of their commander, and not otherwise*, except when there is danger to them or their post being rushed, and no one in authority is present to issue orders.

(iii) When it is necessary to open fire no more rounds will be expended than are absolutely necessary to achieve the object in view. One or two rounds controlled may suffice.

(iv) In all cases the fire must be directed against the persons causing the danger, and not be at random. An order such as 'Five rounds, fire', can only be justified in very exceptional circumstances.

(v) Troops sent into the streets either to assist the police or to deal with persons molesting soldiers should be accompanied by a greater proportion of officers and NCOs than usual.

(e) *Instruction for curfew patrols:-*

(i)   Unauthorised persons found in the streets of Dublin City during curfew hours are liable to arrest, but are not liable to be shot on sight unless seen to be carrying firearms, in which case fire should only be opened if arrest cannot otherwise be effected.

(ii) Curfew patrols have the right to fire on persons acting in such a manner as to jeopardise the safety of the patrol.

(iii) In all cases where fire is opened it must be by order only, and strictly limited to what is necessary to effect the object in view.

Proclamation, 12 May 1921, modified this, as civilians were warned to halt if called on to do so, otherwise they were liable to be shot.

Moves

On 24 July 1920, the 2nd Bn. Duke of Wellington's Regiment was moved by rail to Belfast owing to the local disturbances, and attached to the 1st Division. On 24 August 1920, the battalion returned to Collinstown (north of Dublin). On 6 April 1920, this battalion was sent to England for the coal strike, returning on 8 May.

Expansion of Staff

From 21 November a new Legal Branch was sanctioned for Dublin District Headquarters to deal with civilians.

Transfer of Intelligence to Police

On 27 December a great blow was given to Dublin District by the transfer of the Dublin District Intelligence branch to the police (*see* Intelligence, Dublin District Rebellion, 1919-1920, Appendix A, this book). This happened at a time when our activity was at its highest, and some 500 prisoners were on our hands. For several months offensive operations were hampered as a result of this unfortunate change.

CHAPTER IV

Period: December 1920 to July 1921 (Truce)

Congestion of Prisoners (December)
It gradually became necessary to slacken active military operations. The congestion of prisoners had become the ruling factor. Arbour Hill Detention Barracks, Kilmainham Jail, Mountjoy, and numerous battalion cages did not suffice. The slowness of evacuating the prisoners was an insoluble problem. Complete details had to be recorded in the case of every arrest. Any cases coming under ROIR had to be tried by courts martial. The result of this procedure was to involve all concerned in a mass of correspondence. Much of this work fell upon the Intelligence Staff, but this staff at Dublin District had been transferred to the police or dispersed, and the police had yet no staff of clerks. The result was that the required information from the police necessary for the disposal of the prisoners was not forthcoming. In spite of the most strenuous efforts by all concerned a complete impasse was reached, and active operations had to cease.

Hampered by Legal Procedure
In hostilities of this kind the legal element must be suppressed

41

or stagnation will result. Innumerable courts martial were held, in spite of the detriment to operations caused by the absence of the officers and other ranks required as members or witnesses.

In partisan warfare none but very important cases and capital offences should be tried. All other cases should be classified for internment. There is no other way to achieve successful operations. If operations are to be successful the legal aspect must take second place, and this is a maxim that cannot be overruled when large numbers of arrests are made. In Dublin the average number of prisoners in the hands of the district at this period was about 500.

Military Activities (January 1921)

During January searches were continued on a reduced scale, and further success in the capture of arms and explosives resulted. A more extended system of patrolling was initiated.

All loiterers became liable to be searched (by proclamation). Spasmodic blocks in the main thoroughfares were established by troops or Auxiliaries, with a view to finding arms on the people. These blocks achieved little, as the arms were always handed to the women, who were immune from us. Searches of railway trains were commenced by us. It was suspected that arms and despatches were carried by the railway employees, and although we effected no important captures it was ascertained that this means of transport was rendered more difficult for the rebels on account of our activities.

Leakage of Information

One of the greatest difficulties with which we had to contend was the continued leakage of information. This was due to injudicious talking in some cases, but also to deliberate treachery in others. Numbers of civilians were employed by the Crown forces as clerks; others had entry into barracks for engineer work, telephone repairs, etc. Stringent orders were issued in January to the effect that the Commanding Officer of a barracks would in future be responsible that casual labour men would be watched whilst at work in the barracks.

Rebel Activity (January)

The rebels commenced bombing and sniping attacks on military and police vehicles in Dublin. Meanwhile, the armouring and overhead protection of lorries was being pushed on. An incomplete vehicle carrying a patrol of the 2nd Bn. Berks Regiment was, unfortunately, caught with insufficient covering at the back. Two bombs burst in the lorry, wounding one officer and seven soldiers. Road cutting and ambushes in the country increased. In such cases the troops were instructed to invite the local natives to repair the cuts. But the damage done to many of the bridges was irreparable except by experts.

Road Cuts

Roads and bridges were generally cut in such a way as to allow the narrow native ass cart to pass. Generally the cuts were obvious, but in some cases the damage was disguised to form a trap. A favourite place for a road trench was at a sudden blind road bend.

The result of these activities was to confine our heavy transport to certain roads. Crossley tenders were supplied with strong planks (generally one sufficed) for crossing the obstacles.

Poison

Early in January information was received that the rebels intended to poison beer that might be sold to troops. This did not materialise.

White Cross Fund

Towards the end of January the Sinn Féin White Cross fund was much boomed. This was supposed to be for the destitute, so caused by the direct action of the Crown forces. But the money was largely used to assist rebels on the run and their dependents. By forcing the rebels to go on the run we compelled Sinn Féin to spend on their dependents money that could ill be spared. Later, when this assistance was not forthcoming, considerable discontent resulted.

Cordons

Meanwhile, every endeavour was being made by us to capture the IRA leaders. The police agents concentrated their activities in Dublin in order to follow up these men. Special arrangements were made to cordon areas in the City at short notice and carry out a complete search within the cordons. In co-operation with the Police Intelligence, the first cordon was established about the Four Courts area on the 15-17 January (*see* Appendix V). The search was completed in 36 hours, but the chief quarry (M. Collins) was not found, although several rebels of minor importance were taken. A similar cordon was established and searched on 18-19 February about the area of Mountjoy Square, with indifferent results. The deduction drawn from these operations showed that the extent of an area selected for cordoning must be searchable in twelve hours maximum, otherwise the element of surprise passes, and the quarry finds his way out. Dublin is honeycombed with underground cellars and passages. As a result of these experiences, cordons were restricted to smaller areas. In some cases searches were completed in two or three hours.

Arrest of D. Fitzgerald

In February, D. Fitzgerald, the head of the Propaganda Department, Sinn Féin, was arrested in Dublin. His place was ultimately taken by Erskine Childers. On the 20th another office of Mulcahy's was captured in South Frederick Street. Meanwhile, the attention of the authorities was again directed to certain banks, where ultimately large sums of rebel funds were seized.

Curfew at Trim

Owing to frequent petty outrages in the Trim area, curfew restrictions from 10pm to 5am were put into force in that place on 9 July.

Protection of Cars (March)

Orders were now issued for the protection of military touring cars. At least one armed man must travel as escort to the driver. The car hoods were to be kept up and the seats were to be padded with body armour.

Teeling Escape

Three important civilians escaped from Kilmainham Jail (military custody) on 16 February, with assistance from at least two of the warders. Teeling, one of the fugitives, was awaiting execution for murder.

Military Escorts on Railway Trains

As the result of the breakdown of the railway strike in December, the railways were again being extensively used by the Crown troops. To counteract this the rebels commenced to ambush the trains carrying parties of Crown forces. Special instructions for such military escorts for such military escorts were therefore issued in February (*see* Appendix VI).

Curfew

Owing to continued outrages in the city, on 4 March curfew restrictions were extended to the hours 9pm to 5am in the DMP area (less F Division), and on 31 March to 8pm to 5am.

Successful Captures by the Troops (March)

The month of March was a record one for the capture of rebel arms and munitions in the district, totalling 15 rifles, 54 revolvers, 8 shotguns, 3,440 rounds ammunition, 235 bombs, 814 detonators, and a large quantity of explosives. As a result of these successes the IRA were compelled to alter the distribution, by reducing the size of their dumps and frequent move of dumps became prevalent. Another important capture at this time was that of the Sinn Féin Propaganda Office at Molesworth Street, Dublin.

Convoying Administrative Vehicles

The rebels, meanwhile, continued their activities in bombing and sniping on Crown force vehicles, but without any serious interference to our movements. It became necessary, however, for the usual routine supply transport to be convoyed. For this purpose a section of Peerless armoured cars was put at the immediate disposal of OC, RASC. The armoured cars were invaluable for the work with heavy motor transport in the city and a great saving in manpower.

Burning Vehicles

The rebels now diverted their attacks generally to unescorted vehicles, a sure sign that they had enough of ambushing armed escorts. In most cases they burnt the vehicle and did not harm the drivers.

Curfew

On 3 April, curfew restrictions in Dublin District area were reduced to the hours 10pm to 5am.

Active Service Units

It was during this month (April) that we obtained first definite evidence that 'Active Service Units' had been formed in the IRA. This was good news, showing to what straits they were reduced in order to maintain their activities.

Dug-outs

Information was also received that dug-outs had been constructed in the country for dumps and headquarters.

Activities (Blackhall Place, 29 April 1921)

Some enterprises of minor importance were carried out by both sides during April. The 24th Brigade captured the

Active Service unit of the 1st Bn. IRA, Dublin Brigade at Blackhall Place; some 40 men were taken without resistance. In addition, several dumps were discovered during this period. But our active offensive continued to be hampered in Dublin by congestion of prisoners, dating from the handing over of the Intelligence to the Police in December.

Murder of Loyalists

In the country the murder of Loyalists became prevalent. It was impossible with the facilities at our disposal to give protection to any number of individuals.

Road Cuts – Fairs Stopped

The road cutting continued, and in the Navan, Kells districts, became so prevalent that a Proclamation was issued (26 April 1921) forbidding fairs to be held in the county until the damage to roads ceased. This came into force on 1 May and continued until the Truce. It certainly acted as a deterrent.

Rebels Capture Armoured Car and Enter Mountjoy, 14 May 1921

The rebels commenced considerable activity in the Kingstown district, a hitherto quiet area. But their most brilliant achievement was the capture of an armoured car (Peerless) at the Abattoir, on routine duty. The crew were surprised, and the car was then driven by the rebels in British uniform to Mountjoy Prison, where it was admitted by the warders, under the impression that it had come from Dublin District Headquarters. As regards the military crews of these cars it must be remembered that they were largely composed of young Infantry lads taken from many units, and under the command of camouflaged NCOs. Generally speaking, their work was excellent, but in this case they had become careless and were caught.

The captured car having been driven into the prison by its captors, two disguised as British officers entered the prison buildings. Their object was to release McKeon, obtaining touch with him on the pretext that they were courts martial officers. However, owing to an alarm outside, and the alertness of the military guard, combined with the vigilance of the head warders, they were frustrated. The car, with its occupants, still unrecognised as hostile, was permitted to depart. It was ultimately found abandoned on the outskirts of the city. (Standing orders for Armoured Cars, *see* Appendix IV.)

Interference with Claims

Endeavours were now made by the rebels to interfere with the lodgement of claims by civilians and others against the Irish communities. Without official legal assistance it became difficult to obtain assistance from the Irish bar, and then only at exorbitant fees.

Funds

Attempts were also made by the IRA to obtain money, of which they were always in need, by several means, such as raising the rates and collecting at church doors. In the latter case the work was generally done by women or children and under some assumed charity.

Motor Restrictions Reduced

In April, the time for using motor cars by Permit was increased from 8pm to 9pm, owing to the lengthening of daylight.

'Q' Company, Auxiliary, RIC (Searching Ships)

Complaints had been made (in February) by this headquarters, that effective arrangements were required to search ships at North Wall, Dublin. Previously, the troops had been ordered to carry out these searches, for which they were too inexperienced to be of use. Arrangements were therefore made by the police to raise a special Auxiliary Company ('Q'), composed of officers and men with experience in ships. The Headquarters and bulk of 'Q' Company were located at London and North Western Hotel, North Wall, in April.

Shooting Government Animals

It was during the month of April that the first cases of shooting Government horses occurred. This was carried out against certain unprotected transport vehicle animals. Such outrages by Irishmen caused a considerable stir even amongst their own supporters, and never became very prevalent. Orders were therefore issued that transport and other animals must in future be escorted. This took the form in the case of horse transport of sending out drivers armed, and accompanied by at least one other armed soldier, and as far as possible working in convoys. A proportion of exercise parties also carried arms.

Curfew

On 14 May, curfew restrictions in DMP area were reduced

to between 10.30pm and 4am, owing to the lengthening of daylight.

By the beginning of May the rebel ambushes in the city had somewhat abated. On the outskirts, in the direction of Baldonnel aerodrome, however, endeavours were made to interfere with the RAF traffic, and several rather futile ambushes took place.

Destruction of Government Stores

The policy of destroying Government stores was now noticeable in Dublin. This generally took the form of burning. Special precautions became necessary to protect such stores on arrival by sea or rail. This was rendered all the more difficult in Dublin owing to the short notice received before arrival. In some cases no warning was given.

Despatch Riders

Frequent attacks in Dublin were also made against military despatch motor cycle riders. Few of these were successful, chiefly owing to the gallantry of the riders who carried arms and protected themselves. As the danger became more prevalent, the use of these despatch riders was forbidden, except in special cases, and then riders must work in pairs. The despatch rider routine service was taken over by armoured cars.

Civilians to Halt

On 12 May a Proclamation was issued, warning civilians to halt when called upon by members of the Crown forces. It was found necessary to issue this as a legal protection to the troops in the event of their having to fire at rebels who tried to escape when ordered to halt (*see* Military summary below, orders for firing).

Extensive Search of Trains

In May orders were received from GHQ to co-operate in the search of railway trains on a pre-arranged date. This was with a view to investigating reports that the engine drivers and railway guards were frequently employed in despatch carrying. Although the results of our searches were not encouraging, there is no doubt that this action interfered with the rebel despatch service arrangements.

Mails Searching

The rebels frequently raided the mails, no doubt with good results, as the majority of the Post Office personnel were sympathetic.

In Dublin we seized the mails on two occasions without satisfactory results. On one of these occasions in 1920 one 3-ton lorry load of mails was taken by us. The work of inspecting so many letters was very laborious, some 12 officers were employed for three days. Before mails are seized it is essential that adequate arrangements are ready beforehand for dealing with the letters.

Thomson Machine Gun

On 22 May information was received that the rebels were negotiating with a firm in the USA for the purchase of sufficient Thomson machine guns to supply all units. The issue of these guns was frequently reported, but definite existence of more than two was never obtained in the Dublin District area. These were used in an ambush against a railway train in Dublin on 16 June.

Destruction of Custom House (25 May)

On 25 May the destruction of the Custom House by the active members of the 2nd Bn. Dublin Brigade took place. On 25 May at about 13.10 hours, information was received from DMP that the Custom House had been rushed by approximately 100 civilians. An armoured car was at once despatched, followed by 'F' Company, Auxiliary Division, RIC with another armoured car. The leading armoured car arrived about 13.25, endeavoured to prevent the raiders escaping from the Custom House, and succeeded in covering the southern side. 'F' Company, on arrival, made for the northern side, and were heavily fired on and bombed on reaching the railway bridge, suffering four casualties. About a dozen raiders were seen to run from the Custom House, and were fired on and believed to be hit, but definite report is not to hand. About four minutes later, 'Q' Company, Auxiliary, RIC (from North Wall), who had also been warned, arrived and covered the eastern side of the Custom House. By this time the Custom House was surrounded but in flames.

The Auxiliaries entered the front door of the Custom House and found many revolvers and petrol tins. Some of these were taken out, but owing to the heat of the flames the Auxiliaries were compelled to withdraw.

A large number of civilians came out of the Custom House when it burst into flames, with their hands up; these were all marshalled by the Auxiliaries and head Customs officials were asked to identify their own employees, who were not detained. On completion of identification, about 70 civilians remained, of whom seven showed distinct traces of petrol. These 70 civilians were arrested. Meanwhile, orders had been issued for troops to move from the Royal Barracks and the Castle, those from Royal Barracks (Wiltshire Regiment) being in charge of a field officer, who had orders to take over command of the whole operation. This was done, and arrangements were made to withdraw the Auxiliaries and piquet the area with troops.

The fire brigade arrived and were assisted in their endeavours to extinguish the fire, but the Custom House could not be saved. Intermittent explosions continued, evidently from ammunition and bombs left in the place by raiders.

The casualties that can be definitely reported are 7 civilians killed, 4 auxiliaries wounded, and 10 civilians wounded, one of whom was known to be a raider. The wounded civilians other than the raider were not detained in King George V Hospital. Over 100 civilians were ultimately arrested in this affair. They composed the whole of the active portion of 2nd Bn. Dublin Brigade, IRA.

M. Collins' Headquarters and Austen Stack's Office Captured (May)
Towards the end of May we were successful in capturing M. Collins' headquarters (Mary Street), Dublin, and Austen Stack's office at Molesworth Street. Important documents were seized at both these places.

Increased Destruction of Roads
In the country, owing to the destruction of roads, the question of a greater use of cycles came up. Although in Dublin District area movement had not yet been restricted to this extent, the necessity had to be anticipated. Meanwhile,

captured documents showed that the rebels had been considering the best methods of ambushing cyclist patrols.

Interference with Unarmed Soldiers

In June endeavours were now made by the rebels in Dublin
either to drive unarmed soldiers off the streets or incite them
to commit excesses. Frequent cases occurred where soldiers
were molested. Orders were again issued warning the troops
to keep to the main streets and to walk out in parties.
Increased military and Auxiliary patrols were employed on
such routes during the necessary hours. These precautions
proved adequate.

IRA Reorganise: Use of Dug-outs (June)

It was at this time that evidence was discovered that the
rebels intended to reorganise into Divisions. Principles were
laid down for the establishment of headquarters (in dug-outs),
and the formation of the new headquarters was pushed on.
Their instructions included arrangements for officers, IRA,
to be available continually at the various headquarters, a system of companies taking turn at guard and DR duties was
also foreshadowed.

Destruction of Shell Factory

On the afternoon of 3 June the GHQ Motor Repair and
Ordnance Depot at the Shell Factory, Dublin, caught fire. The
flames spread rapidly, but the most valuable part of the works,
namely the repair shops, was saved. This incendriarism was
undoubtedly the result of treachery, probably on the part of the
civilian employees. The rebels claimed this as a great victory.

Military Activity

Meanwhile, the rebel activities increased. In spite of all efforts no success had been achieved in arresting the IRA chiefs. A general round up of the rank and file was not permitted, nor was our office machinery yet capable of dealing with such a contingency. Rebel activities now took the form of murders of civilians, destruction of government property, enforced contributions from civilians, seizure of public funds wherever possible, and attacks on unarmed soldiers. This displayed a principle of doing as much damage as possible, but not in the face of any danger.

Effective Patrols

To counteract these activities in the city a more intensive system of patrolling was inaugurated by us. Each battalion was allotted an area in which it was responsible for keeping order and patrolling. The method of patrolling was left to the Commanding Officer. Sometimes motor transport was used, others were on foot or cycles, whilst Auxiliaries were used in mufti. But this last method was given up, except in special cases, on account of the danger incurred by the Auxiliaries in clashing with a military patrol and not being recognisable. For special operations Auxiliaries were occasionally dressed in mufti, having uniform hats in their pockets ready to put on at the right moment as a distinguishing mark.

The most effective were the foot patrols, that made sudden surprise appearances by day and lay in ambush by night. The principle of searching suspicious looking individuals proved more effective than general 'hold-ups'. It has since been reported by the IRA leaders that this system of continuous patrolling caused them more trouble than any of our operations in Dublin.

Attacks on Coastguards

The rebels now (June) made a concentrated effort against the coastguards. In most cases the coastguardmen who are Irishmen were disarmed without resistance, and the stations burnt. But beyond the moral effect the military situation did not suffer from these depredations.

Enforcing Curfew

Endeavours had been made to ignore the curfew restrictions in certain areas of the city. The result was that large numbers, up to 100 a night, were arrested. The system of the civil magistrate dealing with curfew cases was always unsatisfactory. His awards did not even act as a deterrent.

Towards the end of June a new scheme was put into practise by the IRA. This was in the form of sniping at guards and patrols during curfew hours in Dublin. Almost nightly, continuous sniping took place round the Custom House and Castle. It was therefore decided that drastic action must be taken by the troops. The population in Dublin were warned that any person even with a pass going out during curfew hours was liable to be shot. At the same time officers were advised not to move out during curfew except on duty. The effect of this was to drive all but armed rebels off the streets during curfew, which facilitated the work of our patrols.

Murder of Lieutenant Breeze

On 19 June Lieut. H. Breeze, 2nd Bn. Worcestershire

Regiment, was brutally murdered by rebels whilst motoring with friends.

Arrest of De Valera and Erskine Childers

On 20 June De Valera was arrested in Dublin by a patrol of the 2nd Bn. Worcestershire Regiment under a false name, owing to incriminating documents being discovered in his house. It was not until arrival at Portobello Barracks that he divulged his name as Mr De Valera, 'President of the Irish Republic'. He was released on the following day after being treated as an officer prisoner and given an officer's quarter. On 9 May Erskine Childers was arrested in Dublin and released in a few hours by the order of the government. It was at this time that the first peace parleys were in progress.

Reinforcements: Protection

On 16 June military reinforcements began to arrive. Some 14 units passed through Dublin either to remain in the district or to proceed to other Divisions. The protection of these troops, which devolved whilst in the district on to Dublin District Headquarters, was difficult. The rebels had determined to do as much damage to them as possible. Railways were mined for troop trains, and snipers were posted. Our precautions were modified as matters developed. The normal arrangement in Ireland for a pilot engine to travel in a different section of the line to its train was obliviously futile. Sometimes a gap of 15 minutes occurred. In one case the railway gangers removed sections of the line during the interval with the object of derailing the troop train. Meanwhile, snipers were waiting in ambush to fire on the derailed train.

Owing to a goods train falling into the trap in error the troops were saved.

In spite of pilot engines running in the same sector as the troop train (all the railway employees except Great Northern Railway were against us), and aeroplanes convoying it, adequate protection was impossible. One train was saved by a military patrol surprising the rebels when mining the line. But it was impossible to watch the lines throughout. The mines were not instantaneous, but controllable by someone on the look out. They could therefore be laid beforehand, and their presence could be made impossible of detection. The reason for seizing keys and batteries of telegraph instruments was now apparent, as the rebels used these for springing their mines. As a result of these experiences the use of troop trains was stopped. Troops marched or travelled by motor transport in tactical formation, whilst their heavier baggage, with escort, used the ordinary passenger trains.

The final procedure adopted in the city for the protection of these troops during their move through it, now by march route, was to piquet certain commanding roofs of houses and patrol the flanks of the route with Crown forces in motor transport. Of the 14 units passed into or through Dublin between May and July, our total casualties were two wounded, so the rebels completely failed to damage the reinforcements; but they were anxious times for us, and several narrow escapes occurred. The only safe method of movement proved to be battalions by march route in tactical formation, with aeroplane assistance, when available, in the country.

26th ('P.') Brigade Formed

On 15 June the three counties Monaghan, Cavan, and Louth were added to Dublin District area. A new Brigade, the 26th, with headquarters at Dundalk, was formed (for composition, *see* Appendix I). A description of these counties is found in the Dublin District Intelligence Report.

Use of Cycles forbidden in County Meath

Owing to no cessation of the outrages and murders in Co. Meath, a proclamation was issued forbidding the use of ordinary bicycles in the county (12 June).

Propaganda

Bundles of leaflets comparing IRA reports with the facts were issued down to detachments for distribution, and also scattered from aeroplanes throughout the country.

IRA Demoralisation

In July it was noticeable that a number of armed civilians, obviously IRA were being captured individually by our patrols without resistance, a sign of further demoralisation in the IRA ranks.

Certainly by this stage the rebels had again begun to realise how hopeless was force. They had been driven to resort from one method to another, and in the final stages to adopt the least dangerous methods to themselves. We were compelled to remain mainly on the defensive during the spring, chiefly through complete congestion of prisoners, as explained above, and later through lack of troops. Our troops were on the whole young and untrained. The personnel of units was continually changing owing to drafts being despatched. In spite of all these advantages, the IRA had been enough by the middle of July, and were ready for the Truce, which was signed on the 11th.

MILITARY SUMMARY
Special Operations

Ticknock Mountain (Wicklow Hills)
Information was received that the rebels had constructed dug-outs in the Wicklow Hills. Aeroplane photographs were taken of certain definite areas which showed signs of such work on the Ticknock Mountain. On 19 June 'C' Coy. Auxiliary RIC piqueted the hill at dawn, and searched the area. One dug-out in process of construction was discovered.

During the period under review several operations of rounding-up villages, camps, drilling and suspected gun-running were carried out, the most important being at Swords, Blanchardstown, Dunboyne, Five Mile Point (Co. Wicklow), Wicklow Hills. None of these operations call for remark. The greatest problem was to effect surprise. Once that was achieved there was little or no resistance.

Armoured Cars
Previous to October 1920, the armoured cars at Dublin District's disposal were two Rolls Royces, six Austins, and three Jeffery Quads. The last named were useless and clumsy. The Austins succumbed to broken back axles, although their work was generally confined to the town. In October 1920, Peerless armoured cars commenced to arrive in batches, and

continued until the end of the year. Additional Rolls Royce cars also arrived, so that by July, 1921, there were four Peerless sections (total, 16 cars) and two Rolls Royce sections of 12 cars at Dublin District's disposal, except for permanent calls on four by GHQ for escort duties to the commander in Chief and mails.

The Rolls Royce cars were manned by Tank Corps personnel. The Peerless crews were a mixture of cavalry, infantry, and artillery men, with RASC drivers. The work of the armoured cars was beyond all praise. A great amount of escort work was taken off the infantry units by them. Recent accounts from IRA leaders show that the rebels had a wholesome dread of our armoured cars. One instance quoted was the panic at the Custom House affair in May, 1921, caused by the unexpected arrival of a Rolls Royce armoured car.

Standing orders for armoured cars were drawn up (*see* Appendix IV), and although one regrettable instance occurred, it was the only case of a car being captured by rebels. A direct attempt was made in 1920, with loss to the attackers.

The Peerless car, with an alert crew, was a difficult problem for the rebels to tackle in a city. Nothing short of a tram car was sufficient to obstruct it.

In the country the cars were liable to be damaged or obstructed by road cuts. Armoured cars were therefore not allowed to proceed unaccompanied by at least one other vehicle, which acted as pilot car.

In cases where an armoured car was moving with one or more vehicles, special measures were required to ensure touch was not lost.

Artillery

Artillery must be prepared to carry out its normal functions in warfare of this type, even in Dublin. Special OPs can be selected beforehand, so that definite points can be shelled from suitable gun positions. Communication with the guns may be a difficulty, but not an insurmountable one. The same applies to heavy artillery. 18-pdr. guns are more use in a city than 4.5 howitzers. The former can be employed for direct fire at short range; that must always be expected under such conditions.

Engineers

There is no field company in Dublin District, but a works company takes its place. The personnel of this company were chiefly employed on accommodation work. For special defences requiring experts much useful work was carried out, such as the protection of Mountjoy, Arbour Hill, and Kilmainham Prisons.

Searchlights

The use of mobile searchlights in conjunction with curfew patrols and raiding parties has already been discussed in Chapter III [of this book]. As methods of curfew patrols altered, and more use was made of surprise and stealth, searchlights were not used so frequently for this work, chiefly on account of the noise caused by the lorry. In cordon work they were invaluable to light up the perimeter and search the roofs of houses and dark areas with their beams.

The two mobile Searchlight Sections (six vehicles, 60cm lights) in Dublin, although at times not fully employed so far as the searchlights were concerned, were indispensable. In partisan warfare of this kind opportunities occur frequently when they are invaluable. But at all times when raiding was in progress by night, the two searchlight lorries equipped with portable lights (by the ingenuity of their own crews) were in demand. All searchlight lorries should be equipped in this way. Another useful improvisation, also due to the initiative of the searchlight personnel, was the attachment of a Lewis gun to a searchlight. The gun and beam moved together, so that fire could be directed with ease and automatically at the place lit up by the beam.

Aldis Lamps

Little opportunity was available to prove the value of the Aldis lamp, owing to their late issue. For raiding purposes they would be invaluable owing to their portability and strong light. Each searchlight lorry should be equipped with at least two Aldis lamps for work in conjuction with the portable lights recommended above. The Adlis lamp is also useful for defence purposes if placed at a sentry post available for use if required. Tactical vehicles should be equipped with at least one Aldis lamp. Special provision is required for recharging these lights (every two weeks). In a large area where battalions are scattered at least one recharging set with trained electrician is necessary for each battalion.

Orders with Reference to Firing on Civilians

(1) If you meet a civilian with arms in his hands, and his intention appears hostile, you are to treat him as an enemy and a traitor to his king and country, and he should be shot. If you can first give him the order "Hands up" without endangering

the lives of yourself and your comrades you are to do so, and bring your rifle to "the charge", and, if he puts his hands up, you will disarm him and make him a prisoner. The first consideration is the safety of yourself and your comrades.

(2) Persons assembled together for the purposes of drilling or rifle practise, *in pursuance of a conspiracy to levy war* against the king, are traitors, and infliction on them of death or bodily harm is not a crime, *only* when it is not possible otherwise:-

(i) To arrest them.

(ii) To re-take and keep them in lawful custody when they have escaped, or are about to escape, from lawful custody, even though they offer no violence.

(3) No shooting will be allowed except by order of an officer, who will give orders for a definite number of rounds to be fired, and will be responsible that his orders are obeyed. The only exception to this order is in the case of a soldier who is out of the reach of an officer, and who must act in accordance with paras. (1) and (2) above on his own responsibility. But the local Commander will be held responsible for permitting unnecessary or promiscuous firing. The number of rounds fired must not be in excess of requirements.

Auxiliary, RIC

In all six Auxiliary Companies ('C', 'F', 'I', 'J', 'N' and 'Q') served in Dublin under military orders. For work in the city and flying columns, thence into the country with motor transport, they were invaluable. With practise they became efficient in co-operation with military operations. Four companies were simultaneously (normally) at Dublin District disposal in the city, and their best work was done there.

Curfew

The establishing of curfew in Dublin had a pacifying effect on the city. On the whole the period of curfew was quiet, and even when sniping commenced during these hours it was only spasmodic and very ineffective. These hours of comparative quiet are invaluable for surprise military operations, for removal of prisoners and other administrative duties.

Intelligent use of the curfew restrictions can also be used as propaganda. It is an onerous restriction that affects the whole population and any relaxation is much appreciated. On the other hand an increase of the restriction for obvious reasons may rouse the public feeling against the perpetrators of the outrages that have caused it.

For many months in Dublin the average number of troops required each night to enforce the restrictions was about three officers and 27 other ranks, the vehicles two 3-ton lorries, and one armoured car. Extra pressure can be put on as required and has generally sufficient moral effect to allow bluff to do the rest.

To make curfew restrictions effective an intelligent watch on the situation generally is essential, especially in a large city like Dublin. Holiday times and weekends required special attention.

The curfew in Dublin was really enforced by pure bluff and a few active silent patrols (rubber-soled shoes).

Summary of Curfew Restrictions in DMP area (less 'F' Division, Kingstown)

Date	Hours
23 February 1920	12 midnight to 5am

Period: December 1920 to July 1921 (Truce)

Date	Hours
30 June 1920	12 midnight to 3am
22 November 1920	10pm to 5am
4 March 1921	9pm to 5am
21 March 1921	8pm to 5am
3 April 1921	10pm to 5am
14 May 1921	10.30pm to 4am
8 July 1921	11pm to 4am

The restrictions were removed on 11 July 1921.

Cages

The question of accommodation for prisoners in the first stage, when numbers are being taken, as in Dublin, requires careful forethought. Otherwise, congestion soon occurs and operations are hampered. Battalions should not be asked to keep their own prisoners for more than twenty-four hours. From battalions the prisoners should be sent to divisional cages. In conditions similar to Dublin the divisional cages should be in three categories. First, a large central cage of 1,000. It is here that the Intelligence personnel function, and from their knowledge can decide where an arrest should be placed. Either he is passed to a cage for special internees, or to another cage for courts martial cases. None of these cages must ever be dispensed with. Intelligence cannot function when prisoners are distributed in numerous battalion cages far apart. Prisoners from the country must remain with units for longer periods owing to distance, but the same principles apply. In the same way GHQ must be prepared to clear all movable prisoners from divisional cages in at the most a week.

Bloodhounds

These dogs must be fully exercised and in the charge of trained men. In a city like Dublin two dogs are sufficient, with at least two men in charge, so that one is always available. Although good results were not achieved, this should not give the idea that bloodhounds are useless. They may justify their existence by one successful bit of work, and it is worth keeping them for that chance.

CHAPTER V

Military Training

Immediately the Truce was signed the troops commenced musketry training. Meanwhile, defensive precautions were maintained, and no vigilance was relaxed. Nine Companies of Infantry proceeded to Kilbride Musketry Camp, one to Ballykinlar from 26th Brigade, and one Cavalry Squadron to the Curragh. This arrangement was kept up until late Autumn, by which time all companies (less one) had been exercised.

On 15 July the 1st Bn. Seaforth Highlanders were sent to assist the 15th Brigade in Belfast, where they remained.

IRA Training

The IRA similarly commenced training. This was done openly, but not on the whole provocatively. Seven training camps were formed in the country round Dublin, the chief being in the Wicklow hills. Each centre consisted of a few tents with a permanent staff in occupation. At the weekends the numbers would swell, in some cases to a few hundred at one centre. Drill, skirmishing, revolver practise, and musketry were carried out. The initial object of this intensive training was probably to keep the IRA occupied and out of trouble. The final object was to have an armed force, with some idea of discipline, available when the peace was ratified.

Cessation of Secret Service

By order of the Government, the Intelligence activities of the police had now to cease. As this Intelligence was the main source that Dublin District Headquarters could depend on, the closing down was a serious matter. The rebel Intelligence abated not at all. Endeavours were made to keep touch with the situation.

Liaison

Actual contact with the IRA was carried on through a Sinn Féin liaison agent in Dublin and, later, one was appointed in each county. The agents in Dublin District were satisfactory, and there was no friction. All dealings were done verbally. A GSO 3 acted as representative for Dublin District, including 24th and 25th Brigades, in Dublin. The 26th Brigade (Dundalk) worked direct with their local agent.

IRA Truculence

As the summer drew on, numbers of recruits were enlisted in the IRA, and a feeling of truculence, chiefly verbal, was encouraged. Sinn Féin police began to come out, and in some cases even interfered with soldiers (unarmed). Much propaganda was spread about having won the war, etc. Civilians were again being intimidated for funds, and accommodation was commandeered. Meanwhile, close touch was kept with the rebel activities. All training camps round Dublin were photographed from the air and reconnoitred. The closing of these camps was regarded as a probable clue to an outbreak. Arrangements were therefore made to report any sign of this.

Chapter V

Danger of Weak Policy (September)

By September, the policy of permitting the rebels to transgress the terms of the Truce was becoming a danger. An ignorant people like the bulk of the IRA really began to believe that they had won the war. Breaches of the truce, especially on the part of Sinn Féin police, became a major menace to peace. Meanwhile, the country was gradually coming under the control of the IRA. In addition, efforts to usurp the functions of local civil government had recommenced, and with success. The police were not encouraged by the Government to interfere. This procedure altered the whole military outlook, especially with regard to detachments in the country. In Counties Meath and Wicklow, small detachments had been originally posted in 1920, as a support to the police, who had not at that time lost all control of their districts.

Control of Country Lost (September)

By September the situation had altered and the country was no longer controlled by the Crown forces. The British Government had permitted the IRA to usurp authority unchecked, and no action by the Crown forces against this procedure was encouraged. Gradually the country was passing under the control of Sinn Féin. The small detachments of Crown forces previously adequate to maintain control were now in danger themselves. The question of concentrating the Crown forces, therefore, became one of urgent necessity.

In September, the kidnapping of civilians became prevalent. Much of this was the work of the Sinn Féin police. Meanwhile, the Belfast boycott was maintained at full pressure.

Departure of Drafts

The situation as described above gradually became more and more acute during the autumn and early winter. To add to the difficulties, large drafts were taken for the East, in November about 4,000 (including one battalion), and in December approximately 1,300 men were moved from the district.

Favourable Change in IRA Leaders (December)

Towards the end of December and beginning of January, an anxiety on the part of the Sinn Féin agency to avoid anything that might cause a breach of the Truce became noticeable. In fact, every endeavour was made to deal with our complaints without delay and effectively.

On 14 January the Treaty was ratified.

Military Summary
Future Operations

Complete new plans for operations based on martial law throughout Ireland were drawn up after the truce commenced.

It was necessary to modify these plans as the number of troops diminished. But arrangements were completed, as far as possible, for taking the offensive immediately.

As the country by the action of the British Government fell into the control of the IRA, so the necessity for withdrawing many detachments became more obvious. Had hostilities broken out, a complete withdrawal to the coast would probably have been desirable, for the above reasons, and on account of the reduction of available troops.

It was decided to earmark certain suitable towns, such as

Howth and Bray, for refugees. RIC detachments would have remained in these places, and the refugees would be armed and organised in conjunction with the police. Refugees would have been billeted on and probably fed by the inhabitants. Should any hitch occur in the feeding arrangement, the towns were convenient for supply from the sea. Where communities of ex-soldiers were in the ascendancy, as at Navan, it was proposed to arm them and use their position also for refugees.

Gun-running

In conjunction with the Royal Navy, arrangements were in hand for the Crown forces to watch the creeks and quays for craft smuggling arms, whilst the Royal Navy patrolled the sea.

Precautions (issued in September)

As regards the peace settlement

The attitude of the extremist element of Sinn Féin is not yet clear, but, in the event of outrages being committed and military action being necessary, the onus for what may ensue must rest without possibility of question on the extremists. The importance of this will be impressed on all officers in command.

The GOC directs that there is to be no relaxation of vigilance. The instructions already issued, with regard to co-operation when called upon by the police in maintaining law and order, will remain in force, and every endeavour will be made to keep in touch with the situation.

Troops and Police

Owing to the rebels gaining control during the Truce period, a concentration of RIC and military detachments was found advisable and carried out in October. Three military detachments were withdrawn and nineteen RIC barracks closed.

For co-operation with the police during the Truce the following instructions were issued:-

In the event of a situation arising during the Truce that calls for military interference, the following procedure will be adopted:-
(a) In the DMP area no action will be taken without reference to Brigade Commanders, who should, if possible, and time permits, refer to the GOC, Dublin District.
(b) In other parts of Dublin District where time permits, the matter should be referred to the Brigade Commanders concerned before action is taken. If time does not permit the local Battalion Commander must use his own discretion. Action by Detachment Commanders subordinate to a Battalion Commander should not be taken with reference, unless absolutely essential for the safety of members of Crown forces.

Reinforcements Sent North
On 15 July, the 1st Bn. Seaforth Highlanders were sent to Belfast, and on 24 September further reinforcements of six Peerless armoured cars were sent, followed by one Searchlight section.

Identification
As explained in the Dublin District Intelligence Report, great difficulty was experienced as regards identifying rebels. Since the Truce we have received reliable information that Michael Collins was arrested on two occasions and Richard Mulcahy

once, when not expected. In all these cases no one was present who knew Collins or Mulcahy by sight, and they were released. Naturally the rebels soon realised our difficulty with regard to identification and played up to it.

Plans (Military)

As already pointed out, our offensive power was always hampered by endless defensive duties, such as guards and escorts. The general scheme had therefore to be modified according to the fluctuations in strength of the troops.

By 11 July 1921, a maximum number of troops were available in Dublin District. New plans were drawn up, under Operation Orders Nos, 1 and 2, with a view to recommencing hostilities if necessary, but this time under martial law, Operation Order No. 2 deals with detail in Dublin city.

Extracts from Operation Order No. 1:-

Summary

It is possible that the rebels suddenly, without warning, may break the Truce by murderous attacks on individual members of Crown forces and concentrated operations against detachments. So long as the members of the Dáil are concentrated in Dublin, and local IRA training camps remain in use, such a contingency is not probable.

It is difficult to realise the object of the rebels in commencing hostilities again, except with a view to carrying out protracted guerrilla operations in Ireland, combined with extensive propaganda aboard, in the hopes of pressure being ultimately brought from outside to compel the British

Government to grant a Republic.

At the commencement, such operations in the Dublin District would probably be based on the policy of endeavouring to draw us from our objectives in Dublin City by concentrated attacks on outlying military and police detachments and the interruption of our communications by cutting all roads, railways and wires.

It is therefore essential that small detachments be prepared to withstand a long siege. Wireless is being installed in detachments as plant and personnel become available. But where these do not exist, battalion headquarters in the country should be prepared to obtain touch with their detachments at least every 48 hours during hostilities. Provided reasonable warning of an attack is received, a favourable opportunity for counter measures by the Crown forces should result. Brigade and battalion mobile reserves are therefore essential.

Each brigade in Dublin will retain a reserve of at least a battalion for operations in and around Dublin, together with a mobile reserve of Auxiliaries.

Battalion Commanders in the country must realise that their object is to hold their own without assistance from elsewhere. These detachments of troops and police, although undesirable from a military point of view, are essential for political reasons, which must predominate in warfare of this kind.

It may, however, be necessary to concentrate the RIC more than at present, especially in the 26th Brigade area.

Intention
In the event of a resumption of hostilities the GOC intends to act as follows:-

(a) Interrupt the IRA communications in Dublin. Arrest as many members of the Dáil as possible and break up the Dublin Brigade, IRA, by wholesale arrest of known members. Search for arms and munitions.

(b) Outside of Dublin maintain existing detachments, which will take the offensive by -

    (i) Arresting known members of the IRA.

    (ii) Searching for local IRA headquarters, arms and munitions.

    (iii) Interrupting IRA communications.

Transition Stage

The initial phase will thus consist of operations by the Crown forces under Restoration of Order in Ireland Regulations (so far as Dublin District is concerned), which can be put into force within a few hours.

The proclamation of martial law must take time, and its effect will be to unify the action of Crown forces and extend their powers over the civilian population.

Precautions

From the receipt of the code word:-

(a) No officer or other rank will be permitted to move from the protection of troops except with an adequate escort. If vehicles are required, at least two will be used together in all parts of Dublin District except Dublin City, where one armoured car or armoured 3-ton lorry will suffice.

(b) Correspondence must therefore be reduced to absolute essentials, and every effort be made to utilise existing patrols and convoys, where feasible, to assist in DR duties.

List of Appendices
(Issued with O/O No. 1 and not included here.)

Appendix I	Description of D/D Brigade Areas and Distribution of Troops
Appendix II	Proclamations.
Appendix III	Legal Powers.
Appendix IV	Administrative Arrangements.
Appendix V	Medical Arrangements.
Appendix VI	Disposal of Prisoners.
Appendix VII	Communications.
Appendix VIII	Co-operation with Aircraft.
Appendix IX	Fighting Equipment, Reserves and Establishments of Munitions, Supplies and RE Stores.
Appendix X	SOS Signals (Rockets, etc.)

The intention described above had been the same throughout the period of hostilities. By Easter, 1920, the objective had been generally gained in Dublin District but was lost by the release of the hunger strikers. By the end of December we were again approaching final success. The proclamation and enforcing of martial law throughout Ireland at this period might have had decisive results. For political reasons it was considered necessary to transfer Dublin District Intelligence to the police, with the immediate result that our offensive had to slacken at this vital period.

By 11 July, 1921, the IRA formations had been virtually broken up as such, and many leaders were in our hands. The IRA as an army had ceased to exist, and were reduced to bands of ruffians who, sooner or later, were bound to fall into our hands. Drastic shooting, after a quick and decisive trail, for certain offences was *all* that was required to end the matter for the time being but that was all.

Conclusions

The rebels may fairly claim at some future date to have retained a large force of British troops in the neighbourhood of Dublin.

Dublin was, and is, the heart and soul of the whole conspiracy. It was the principal military base for all Ireland, also the headquarters of the Viceroy and the Commander in Chief, as well as the site of large and important military stores of explosives and arms.

In spite of the initial determined opposition by large numbers of men, backed up by a sympathetic or frightened population, law and order was maintained in no uncertain fashion throughout. No military reverse worth considering was sustained, although operations were carried out by a few battalions of young soldiers, many of whom had hardly fired a rifle, and all units much under strength, with little or no training.

In addition, military operations were hampered at every turn by legal technicalities, political considerations, the absence of any organisation capable of identifying wanted men, the difficulty of organising a Secret Service during active operations, and the almost complete absence in Dublin of police support with regard to political crime.

Above all, the vital power of martial law, i.e., summary execution for certain offences, was completely absent.

Nevertheless, at the time of the Truce, in spite of every

difficulty and all propaganda, the IRA in Dublin District, although under the immediate eyes of what remained of their Headquarters' staff was reduced to a condition which can only be described as "cowardly, cunning and contemptible". This expression describes their operations in the district as a whole, when consideration is given to the enormous resources at their command and the difficulties with which we had to contend.

The *coup de grace* might have taken a little longer, but, *given real power*, it was inevitable.

It has been recently ascertained that by the middle of July 1921, the strength of the IRA throughout Ireland was 80,000 men, of whom one-third were armed. The difficulties of ammunition supply had become acute, the average at this time being only five rounds per weapon.

Appendix I

Composition of Dublin District Allocation of Battalions

1. January 1920 to March 1920

1st Bn. King's Own Royal Regiment	Richmond Barracks
1st Bn. Prince of Wales' Volunteers	Wellington Barracks
2nd Bn. Prince of Wales' Volunteers	Richmond Barracks
1st Bn. Wiltshire Regiment	Royal Barracks
2nd Bn. Royal Berkshire Regiment	Portobello Barracks
2nd Bn. Worcestershire Regiment	Portobello Barracks
1st Bn. East Surrey Regiment	Collinstown
51st Bn. Welch Regiment	North Dublin Union
52nd Bn. Sherwood Foresters	Ship Street Barracks

2. March 1920 to December 1920

(a) 24th (P.) Brigade

1st Bn. East Surrey Regiment	Collinstown
(relieved by 2nd Bn. D of WR in June 1920)	
1st Bn. Lancashire Fusiliers	North Dublin Union
1st Bn. Wiltshire Regiment	Royal Barracks
2nd Bn. Worcestershire Regiment	Portobello Barracks

Expansion in month of June 1920
1st Bn. South Wales Borderers (Co. Meath)

(b) 25th (P.) Brigade

1st Bn. King's Own Royal Regiment	Richmond Barracks
2nd Bn. Prince of Wales' Volunteers	Richmond Barracks
1st Bn. Prince of Wales' Volunteers	Wellington Barracks
2nd Bn. Royal Berkshire Regiment	Portobello Barracks

Expansion in month of June 1920
1st Bn. Cheshire Regiment (Co. Wicklow) 5th Brigade, RGA (Tallaght). (Divisional Troops.)

Editor's Note: The 2nd Bn. Prince of Wales Volunteers was relieved by the 2nd Bn. Welch Regiment in June, 1920.

3. DECEMBER 1920 TO JULY 1921
REINFORCEMENTS
(a) 24th Brigade
15 January 1921

2nd Bn. E. Surrey Regiment	Marlborough Hall

16 June 1921

2nd Bn. Royal West Kent Regiment	Phoenix Park NDU

7 July 1921

1st Bn. Seaforth Highlanders	Phoenix Park

(On 30 July 1921, 1st Bn. Seaforth Highlanders are sent Belfast)

(b) 25th Brigade
28 December 1920.

3rd Bn. Rifle Brigade   Ballsbridge
5 July, 1921.
1st Bn. Loyal Regiment   Portobello Barracks
Note:- 3rd Bn. Rifle Brigade, [transferred] to 24th Brigade, April 1921; 2nd Bn. Worcestershire Regiment, [transferred] to 25th Brigade, April 1921.

(c) 26th Brigade (Dundalk)
July 1921
1st Bn. King's Royal Rifle
Corps   Co. Monaghan
2nd Bn. King's Own Yorkshire
Light Infantry   Co. Louth
2nd Bn. Middlesex Regiment   Co. Cavan
33rd Brigade, RFA   Dundalk

(d) DIVISIONAL TROOPS (Infantry)
2 July, 1921
2nd Bn. Duke of Cornwall's
Light Infantry   Richmond Barracks

Dublin Castle
4. DIVISIONAL TROOPS
(a) RAF
    'C' Flight, 100 Squadron,
    RAF   Baldonnell
(b) Cavalry
    15th Hussars   Marlborough Barracks
(c) RFA
    33rd Battery, RFA   Marlborough Barracks

(d) R.G.A.

5th Brigade, RGA	Tallaght

(e) R.E.

D/D Signal Company, H.Q.	Dublin Castle
GHQ Signal Company	Marlborough Barracks
'K' Signal Company	Alderborough House
Det. 14 Survey Company	Mountjoy Barracks
No. 1 Works Company	Beggars Bush Barracks
No. 1 Mobile Searchlight Group HQ	Beggars Bush Barracks
1 Section, M. Searchlight Group	Dublin Castle
Mobile Wireless Section	GHQ, Ireland

(f) Tanks

No. 5 Armoured Car Company	Marlborough Barracks

(less 2 Brigade Peerless Sections).

1 'RR' Section	Dublin Castle
1 'P' Section, RASC	Royal Barracks

(g) RASC

615 MT Company	Royal Barracks
1157 MT Company	Shell Factory
1167 MT Company	Collinstown
22nd MT Company	Royal Barracks
25th MT Company	Royal Barracks
'D' Supply Company	North Dublin Union
'BB' Remount Company	Island Bridge
'CC' Remount Company	Lusk

(h) RAMC

No. 14 Company	King George V Hospital

Composition of Dublin District – Allocation of Battalions

(i) RAOC

No. 14 Company   Island Bridge Depot

(j) RAVC

Veterinary Hospital   Arbour Hill Barracks

(k) Aux. RIC

'F' Company   Dublin Castle

APPENDIX II

List of Casualties, 21 November 1920

Killed

Rank	Name	Unit
Major	Dowling, C.M.C.	General List (late of the G Guards Res. of Officers)
Captain	Price, L.	General List (late Middlesex Regt.)
Captain	Baggallery, G.T.	Extra Regimentally Employed List DDHQ, RO
Captain	Newberry, W.F.	Royal West Surrey Regiment DDHQ, RO
Lieutenant	Maclean, D.L.	General List (late Rifle Brigade)
Lieutenant	Ames, A.	General List (late G Guards, SR)
Lieutenant	Bennett, G.	General List (late RASC, MT)
Lieutenant	Angliss, H.	General List

| | Morris, C.A. | RIC |
| | Garniss, F. | RIC |

Wounded

| Lt-Colonel | Montgomery, H.F. | Royal Marine Light Infantry GHQ. |

Died of wounds

| Lt-Colonel | Woodcock, W.J. | Lancashire Fusiliers |
| Lieutenant | Murray, R.G. | General List (late Royal Scots, TF) |

Died of wounds

| Captain | Keenlyside, B.C.B. | Lancashire Fusiliers |

Appendix III

Dublin District Standing Orders for Armed Parties Moving by Lorry and Lorry Convoys

Part 1. General

1. The term 'lorry' in these orders includes all vehicles of 15 cwt. carrying capacity and upwards.

2. No armed party or escort will consist of less than one officer or selected NCO, and six men. The maximum number on one lorry will not exceed one officer or NCO and twelve other ranks, except when it is necessary in an emergency to convey a greater number for a special duty and no additional transport is available. In this case at least one lorry must be properly manned, so that the men on it have sufficient space for fighting purposes.

3. Rifles will have magazines charged and safety catches back. A round will not be placed in the chamber, except in the case of men detailed for 'immediate action', *vide* paras. 5 and 6.

4. Revolvers and pistols will be loaded. (Automatic pistols will not have a round in the chamber and the mechanism will be set at 'safe').

5. Normally, bayonets will not be fixed, but it is left to the

discretion of Brigade Commanders to modify this order if they should consider it necessary.

6. Every lorry which carries armed personnel will have the following minimum number specially told off for duty, and for immediate action:-

    (a) A forward 'look out', sitting beside the driver.

    (b) Two side 'look outs', one on each side of the lorry.

    (c) A rear 'look out' by the tail-board.

7. All 'look outs' mentioned above will have their revolvers or rifles ready for 'Immediate action'. In the case of rifles, 'Immediate action' will mean that a round is in the chamber with the safety catch back, the rifle being held muzzle pointing up, the barrel resting, if desired, on the side or tail-board of the lorry.

8. All 'look outs' in lorries will stand or sit in such a position that they can use their rifles without delay. The sides of the tarpaulin hood will always be rolled up to allow for this.

9. In addition to the 'look outs', one or two men will be told off specially to drop the tail-board of the lorry if required.

10. A NCO or selected private will be detailed to command the party inside the body of each lorry. Should there be only one NCO on the lorry, he will be in the body of the lorry and not on the seat beside the driver.

11. The officer, NCO, or selected private in command in the body of the lorry will be responsible that the 'look outs' are posted, that they are always on the alert, and that reliefs are arranged.

12. NCOs and men not detailed for the above-mentioned duties will hold their rifles in their hands, and may be allowed to sit down if there is room.

13. Look outs, officers, and NCOs in command of troops in lorries must always, when away from barracks, be suspicious of harmless looking parties of civilians on the roadside. In several cases parties of civilians playing 'pitch and toss' have suddenly produced revolvers and held up our patrols and lorries. Groups of civilians sitting by bridges with steep approaches thereto will also be watched closely.

14. In case of hostile attack or ambush, the 'look outs' will immediately open fire from the lorry, whilst the remainder will get down as quickly as possible and go for the enemy.

15. The officer or NCO in command will impress on all ranks before starting off on a lorry journey that, in the case of an ambush being met with, it is essential that there should be quickness, obedience to orders, and complete absence of panic. Rapid fire from the 'look outs' will greatly disconcert the enemy, and will give the remainder of the party time to get out and counter-attack.

16. 'Lorry drill', *i.e.*, action to be taken if ambushed, will be practised on every possible occasion, and this drill is to be *rehearsed either before the start, or soon after the start at some quiet part of the road by each party or escort*. As a precaution against hostile fire from behind hedges, banks, or walls along the roadside, certain men will be detailed *before starting* for the duty of getting through or over the hedges, etc., on both sides of the road, and thus enfilading the enemy.

17. Should the lorry break down on the road an isolated party of troops will be specially on its guard against attack. Civilians are not allowed to collect near the lorry, and will only be allowed to pass by in twos and threes at good intervals. Should there be a hedge or wall by the roadside some of the party will

be so stationed as to cover the far side. An *unarmed* man will be sent to the nearest detachment or police barracks for assistance in the case of a serious breakdown to the lorry.

18. It is better to appear ridiculous in the eyes of civilians by over-caution than risk the lives of your men or loss of rifles and ammunition.

19. (a) *All tactical lorries will carry:-*

> One pick.
>
> One shovel.
>
> One wire hawser (for towing purposes, or for dragging away obstructions).
>
> One hand axe.
>
> One cross-cut saw.
>
> One pair wire cutters.
>
> One crowbar.
>
> Four planks (for use as wheel bases, to allow the lorry to cross over the filled-in earth of any trench dug across the road).
>
> Three trench mortar bombs, with slow fuses.

(b) *In the Dublin Metropolitan area*, including Kingstown and Dalkey, lorries other than tactical lorries will carry:-

> One wire hawser.

(c) *Outside the Dublin Metropolitan area.*

> (i) Lorries, other than tactical lorries employed in rushing troops out to meet an emergency, will, at the discretion of the Officer Commanding on the spot, carry all, any, or none of the stores in para. 19 (a), according to the urgency of the call and the time available.
>
> (ii) In any convoy conveying troops, prisoners, or stores, at least one lorry will carry the stores enumerated in

para. 19 (a). subject to sub para. 19 (c) (i).

20. Officer and NCOs in command of lorry parties and escorts must be prepared to meet the following road obstacles:-

(a) Trees felled across the road.

(b) Stone walls across the road.

(c) Trenches (covered with camouflage material or left open).

(d) Barbed wire entanglements.

Instructions for the removal of (a) have already been circulated.

21. Every lorry carrying troops will be provided with a cover as a protection against bombing. This cover must not prevent a clear view from the sides.

22. Instructions will be posted up in all lorries explaining how to stop the lorry if the driver should become a casualty, and in every armed party travelling by lorry there must be at least one soldier who is capable of stopping the lorry if the driver should become disabled.

23. Arrangements are being made to provide armour for tactical lorries, and it is hoped that this work will shortly be completed.

24. The attention of all ranks is directed to this Office letter No. 242/4 S.T., dated 12 July 1920, with reference to the proper use of motor transport vehicles.

25. If two or three lorries are moving in convoy, one lorry will act as advanced guard, keeping about 200 yards ahead of the others. The escort to be divided between the front and rear lorries.

26. (a) With more than three lorries a convoy will have an advanced guard lorry, moving 200 yards in front of the main body. The main body will move close up, with 20 yards distance between each lorry.

(b) If a motor cycle (preferably a combination cycle) is available, it will be utilised as a vanguard 100 yards in front of the advanced guard lorry. An additional motor cycle, if available, should be used for the purposes of communication. If no motor cycle is available and the country is suitable for cycling, a few cyclists can be used with advantage as a vanguard.

27. The strength of the escort will depend on the size and importance of the convoy.

28. The forward 'look outs' and rear 'look outs' respectively, will pass back and forward the usual military signals, such as 'Halt!'; 'Enemy in sight', etc. Rear 'look outs' will be responsible for reporting at once any stoppage or opening out on the part of the following lorries, and when overtaking vehicles require to pass.

29. The officer (or NCO) commanding the convoy escort will be in tactical command of the whole convoy, including the drivers of the vehicles and any other personnel travelling in the convoy. He will travel with some of the escort in the leading lorry of the main body, himself being *inside* the lorry. He will be responsible:-

(a) For the safety of the convoy, and that all military precautions are taken.

(b) That each lorry containing armed personnel is under the command of a NCO, or selected private, and that the 'look outs' are posted before starting.

(c) That all ranks receive instruction before starting as to their action in case of attack, and that such action is rehearsed.

(d) That the convoy moves in the formation laid down,

and that lorries are not left behind. Halts are unnecessary except for meals and purposes of that nature, unless required by the ASC for mechanical reasons.

(e) That the convoy does not exceed a maximum speed of 12 miles per hour on the open road, slowing down to 8 miles per hour when passing through towns and villages. The speed of the convoy should be that of the *slowest* vehicle. *Low-speed vehicles should be at the head of the main body of the convoy*, but if necessary, the high speed vehicles in a convoy may be moved in bounds to cover the advance of the remainder of the convoy, so long as the high and low speed portions of the convoy are each provided with an adequate escort.

(f) That in the case of a lorry breaking down completely (i.e., that it cannot be towed), he shall have transferred to other lorries all its moveable stores. He will use his discretion as to whether he can spare a guard over the broken down lorry until it can be brought in. In any case the driver (unarmed) of the lorry must remain with it.

(g) That he keeps a log of any incidents which may happen on the journey, and that he reports on arrival at his destination to the proper quarter.

30. A copy of these orders will be in the possession of every officer, and Commanding Officers will be responsible that these orders are made known to all ranks. Commanding Officers, or Officers Commanding detachments at the departure point will ensure that the officer or NCO in command of the convoy or lorry party is thoroughly acquainted with his duties.

Appendix IV

Battalion Standing Orders for Armoured Cars in Ireland

General Instructions

1. Every officer, NCO, and private soldier must realise that while on patrol he is liable to sudden attack by armed men when least expected, who will endeavour to overpower him and capture his armoured car, and all ranks, when out on duty on the armoured cars, must not relax their vigilance for one moment, and, in the event of any attempt to attack or rush the car, they will deal with it exactly as if on active service, and without hesitation. The loss of an armoured car will always be a court martial offence.

2. Standing orders will be strictly complied with.

3. Cars must not fall into the hands of the enemy. If all the crew become casualties, they must contrive to put the car and armament into such a state that it cannot be moved by the enemy before assistance arrives.

4. Every officer, NCO, and private soldier is put on his honour that he will fight for his car as long as he is able, and that on no account will he surrender it to the enemy.

5. All members of the crew will invariably be equipped in fighting order and carry revolvers, which will be loaded with six rounds and six rounds in the pouch.

6. Routine duties which are performed regularly are particularly dangerous, and extra precautions must be taken on all occasions by crews performing these duties.

7. When stationary, all doors and flaps will be kept shut except for one gunner, who will keep a sharp look-out, and the car will be closed down for "action". Cars will not remain stationary except when necessary. When stationary in any strange place, except a properly defended military barracks, the engine will be kept running, but well throttled down to avoid petrol waste.

8. Armoured cars will not remain stationary at crossroads, road junctions, or in front of any point (alley, gateway, etc.) from which a sudden attack might be made.

9. If there is a number of civilians standing about in any place where an armoured car has to wait, the crew will take care that the civilians are not permitted to approach within ten yards of the car, and the gunners will keep them covered with their guns.

10. If necessary, the armoured car should draw away to a distance of 25 yards from civilians, etc., so that the gunners can depress their guns sufficiently to cover them.

11. All persons approaching an armoured car, even though in military or police uniform, will be treated with suspicion, and will be considered guilty of intentions to capture the car until they have very definitely and conclusively proved their identity. Rebels are in possession of officers' and men's uniforms, and they use them.

12. In the event of any rush or attack on the armoured car, the driver will immediately get his car moving and draw away from the attacking party, and thus allow the gunners freedom to

shoot with good field of fire. The gunners will act under the orders of the officer i/c car or, if he is not there, under the orders of the senior NCO or private. On no account will any attempt be made by anyone to go to the help of or rescue any person or member of the crew outside the car or leave the car until the attack has been successfully dealt with by the gunners.

13. The officer or NCO i/c car will not leave the car except under very exceptional circumstances; he will then inform the next senior of his intention and will close the door after him.

14. Not more than one officer or man is to leave the car at any one time, and there are ALWAYS to be two gunners in the turrets of the Peerless armoured cars, and one gunner in the turret of the Rolls Royce cars, ready for action.

15. If for any reason the officer or NCO i/c car should have to get out, he must see that the door is fastened. No one will leave the car until it has been ascertained that all is clear, and no suspicious characters are near.

16. Drivers of cars will take orders only from the officer or NCO in charge of the car, or the officers under whose orders he was placed before proceeding to the scene of operations.

17. No smoking is allowed inside an armoured car or within 10 yards of one by soldiers or civilians.

18. Cars will be locked up before being left in military or police barracks.

19. The gun turrets and mountings must be kept well oiled to allow for quick movements of the guns.

20. All members of the crew must be prepared to use their revolvers on raiders if they should manage to get close up to the car.

21. Cars are not to leave barracks without first reporting to

the Section office.

22. Drivers are responsible that the full complement of tools is carried on all occasions.

23. Accumulators are to be tested at least twice a week by the drivers, and entries made in their log books as to their condition. Distilled water is only to be used.

24. The self-starter will only be used in extreme cases and must always be connected, and must be tested every week.

25. Spare petrol must not be carried on the back of any car.

26. Overalls are to be worn on all working parades and while on duty with the armoured cars.

27. Every car must be kept off the road at least one day in every seven for through cleaning and overhaul.

28. In case of an accident, armoured cars must always stop and obtain names and addresses of all persons concerned and of any witnesses to the accident. On returning to barracks the accident will immediately be reported to the Section officer, and a report made out on the accident forms (A.F., W. 3676-four copies) by the driver of the armoured car. In addition, the driver will write a detailed report on foolscap paper (four copies), and reports will be written on foolscap paper (four copies) by the other members of the crew who were present when the accident occurred. When all reports have been made out, they will be handed to the Section officer without delay, and he will immediately forward them to the Commander of his company.

29. Under no circumstances will petrol of any grade be used for cleaning an armoured car owing to danger of fire. Paraffin is issued for this purpose and must only be used.

30. Any rumours of impending attack by the rebels, no matters

from what source or, however unlikely, are to be immediately reported to an officer, preferably one of your own officers, and all the persons likely to be implicated must be warned; no information of this sort is to be ignored.

31. Every care must be taken to safeguard arms and ammunition, and all the instructions issued must be carefully complied with. All officers and .NCOs are responsible that their men are well acquainted with all orders on this subject.

32. Three field dressings must be carried on every armoured car, in addition to those which must be carried by the crew on their persons. Every officer and man must always carry a field dressing on his person.

33. An officer or Section sergeant will carry out daily the following inspection prior to the car leaving barracks:-

(a) Inspect the guns and see that they are properly loaded, and that the water jackets on the Vickers are filled with water.

(b) Inspect revolvers and see that every man has six rounds in his revolver and six in his pouch.

(c) Inspect revolver ports, prisms and all flaps, and see that they move freely and are clean.

(d) See that the gunners have the hand extractors and dismounting wrench in ammunition rack in the turret of the Peerless, and the clearing plug in the Rolls Royce car, ready for use.

(e) See that each Rolls Royce car is carrying an extra Hotchkiss gun.

(f) Inspect all ammunition and belts in the car.

34. Before proceeding on escort duty the officer or NCO i/c car will ensure that he receives instructions as to route and

duty, and that the officer i/c column is informed of the speed limit of the armoured car.

35. No other person except the authorised driver will drive an armoured car except by permission of the Section Commander.

Special Instructions for the Peerless Armoured Cars

1. The crew of a Peerless armoured car consists of one officer or NCO (not below the rank of corporal) in charge, two gunners, one first driver and one second driver.

2. No car will go out without its full crew.

3. The following ammunition will always be carried on the car:-

4 boxes of 24 belts of 50 rounds each	1,200 rounds
1 box SAA in bulk (sealed)	1,000 rounds
12 rounds per man .455	60 rounds
In bulk .455	40 rounds

4. Gunners will have their heads *only* through the opening in the turret, and will not expose more than their heads. One gun will point to the front and one gun to rear.

5. The rear driver must always have his revolver drawn and rear flap open sufficiently high to allow him to get a lookout. All prisms must be kept clean.

6. Cars to be kept clean and sufficiently lubricated. Chains, springs and shackle pin greasers must always be well filled.

7. The lower part of the front driver's flap must always be kept up. The driver's side flap must only be opened at an angle of 45 degrees.

8. Hotchkiss guns will always be loaded, locking handle at safety.

Special Instructions for Rolls Royce Armoured Cars

1. The crew of a Rolls Royce armoured car consists of one

officer or NCO (not below the rank of corporal) in charge, one driver, one gunner.

2. No car will go out without its full crew.

3. The following ammunition will always be carried in the car:-

Vickers gun

3 boxes of 250 rounds	750 to 1,000 rounds
1 belt of 250 rounds on gun	250 rounds

Hotchkiss gun

1 box of 6 belts of 50 rounds	300 rounds

Revolver

12 rounds per man in car	36 rounds
In box	64 rounds

4. Cars, whenever possible, will carry two spare wheels.

5. Tyres must be kept at a pressure of 95 lb. per square inch on the Scsraeder gauge for rear wheels, and 85 lb. for front wheels, subject to tyre, weather and road conditions.

6. Cars to be kept clean and sufficiently lubricated according to Rolls Royce handbook.

7. When on escort duty, cars must regulate their pace to suit themselves, and not use excessive speed in order to keep up with the vehicle being escorted; it must regulate its pace to that of the armoured car.

8. Under no circumstances will the speed of an armoured car exceed 20 miles an hour. Officer or NCO i/c will be held responsible for any accident that may occur to, or be occasioned by, their cars while travelling at excessive speed unless they have received a written order from a superior officer, who will forward a written report to the Company Commander immediately, giving details of the necessity of exceeding the speed limit.

9. Officers and NCOs i/c cars must check the speed of cars and report non-compliance with orders at all times.

10. Drivers must, on return to garage, examine their tyres for glass, nails flints, etc., which may be embedded in the tread, and remove same.

11. If a tyre punctures, the gunner must remain inside the car ready for action.

12. Cars will be started once a week from the inside with the hand-starter.

13. The Officer or NCO in charge of car is responsible that no one sits outside the car except those authorised to do so by Company Headquarters. Persons authorised must be properly dressed, and will be warned that they may not smoke or behave in slovenly manner.

14. Armoured cars will always keep at least 50 yards distance from each other, or 10 yards behind vehicles that they are escorting.

15. Safeguarding of arms on Rolls Royce armoured cars:-

(i) Revolvers will only be left on armoured cars by the order of the Section Commander. Failing such order all revolvers will be handed back into the Section Store on completion of duty.

(ii) When revolvers are on armoured cars, except when on duty, they will be invariably locked up on the chain issued for this purpose to each car. The officer or NCO in charge of car is responsible that this is done on completion of duty, and that the key is in possession of first driver *or* that all revolvers are returned to store.

(iii) In addition, when revolvers are left on armoured cars on the chain, the first driver will ensure that all doors are securely fastened and all port holes closed and pinned.

APPENDIX V

Instructions for Raiding and Searching an Extended Area of Houses in Dublin

29.1.21 [Document date]
The principles will be applied to all searches where applicable in Dublin District area.

1. Operation

The operation should be divided into two parts under different commanders, namely:-
Troops for:-

    (a) Forming the cordon.

    (b) Searching houses.

The first task is to surround completely the area to be searched with a cordon of troops as secretly and rapidly as possible by day or night.

    The second task is to carry out the house to house search, and should normally be executed by daylight.

2. Cordon

    (a) *Time*:- Where troops are prepared for an operation of

this type, provided that necessary stores are available and troops and transport are comparatively concentrated, three hours should be allowed from the time orders reach the OC, cordon troops, to the hour that the troops will leave barracks. This will enable detailed orders to reach all cordon officers concerned.

The time required to establish the cordon will be that required to reach the allotted points on the area to be enclosed plus a few minutes to establish the cordon.

(b) *Method of approach*:- On foot or cycle for the last half mile, and by convergent routes. Searchlight lorries should arrive on the heels of the infantry.

(c) *Distribution*:- (based on a three days' task, and including reliefs.)

The number of troops required cannot be estimated by the extent of the perimeter, but must depend on the number of defiles. The proportion of officers can be reckoned by the extent of the perimeter. The following are given as a guide:-

At bridges and important crossroads   15 other ranks
At ordinary crossroads.   10 other ranks
At a road junction   6 other ranks

Also to prevent movement across the boundary streets of the cordon:-

Two men to 30 yards, without searchlight
Two men to 50 yards, with movable searchlight
Two men to 75 yards, with permanent or continuous searchlight

The proportion of officers:-

One Cordon Section Commander and two officers to assist for each 600 yards of perimeter.

Note:- If operations are continued beyond three days, and the extent of the cordon remains unchanged, the above estimates should be increased 50 per cent.

(d) *Wiring*:- The whole cordon should be wired unless a natural obstacle exists, the wire being erected on the side of the street away from the area to be searched. The type of wiring must vary according to circumstances, but two or three single strands of barbed wire, tied to lampposts or doors of houses, forms a useful obstacle. Scaffolding, tripods, plane wire and barbed wire, concertina coils or *chevaux de frises* are useful for road blocks.

Special wiring parties must be detailed, one to each face of the cordon, each party consisting of one officer and 12 other ranks, divided into two groups of six men each. Each group can run a double strand of wire as described above, down a street at the rate of 100 yards in five minutes, provided light exists (searchlight or otherwise).

A reserve of wire is required for use as the cordon moves forward; meanwhile the original wire concerned should be rolled up and becomes available for further move. Pick-handles are required for rolling up wire, as drums become broken.

(e) *Stores* for cordon troops:-
  Wiring gloves and wire cutters.
  Staples and mallets.
  (For each group of wirers)
  Pick-handles for rolling up wire.
  Reserve of wire (one coil as issued in Dublin contains about 100 yards).
  Sandbags

(f) *Restrictions* will be stringent; the following privileges are therefore issued as a guide, and must be given very sparingly:-

(i) It is sometimes necessary to allow for food and especially milk to be brought into the cordoned area. Children should be allowed to carry out these functions. Any tradesman allowed in for feeding purposes will be accompanied by a soldier.

(ii) Priests and doctors should only be allowed to pass in case of death or serious illness.

(iii) It may be necessary to allow shopowners to pass into the area to open their shops.

(iv) Workmen should be allowed to pass *out* for essential trades. If required, a certificate showing cause for delay should be given to each applicant.

(v) Special facilities for feeding and watering of animals located within the cordon may be necessary.

All persons must pass through an examining post.

Doors and windows of buildings outside of, but adjacent to, enclosed areas will be kept closed to prevent sniping.

(g) *Passes*:- A specimen signature of the Permit officer will be issued to examining posts beforehand. This officer will have his office adjacent to an examining post; out and return passes will be issued by him (forms required).

Persons requiring to enter the cordon without a pass will state their case to the examining post officer and, if adequate, be sent under escort to the permit officer, where a pass will be issued.

All persons passing the examining post will sign their names in a book each time they pass in and out, so that their signature can be checked. The passbook should be alphabetic, and each page divided into several columns, so that a signature can be easily checked.

(h) *Examining posts*:- When adequate, one; otherwise two examining posts will be established in charge of a selected officer, who will be assisted by special police for identification purposes.

Examining posts will be closed during silent hours and for tactical purposes.

All persons, military or otherwise, will only be admitted through an examining post, and the former must show a military pass if not known.

(i) *Miscellaneous:- Searchlight*s:- two searchlights are required for a rectangular area where boundary streets are straight, otherwise more searchlights are necessary, and during the long hours of darkness relief searchlights are required.

Armoured cars are more useful by day than by night, although a reserve of one or two is useful by night.

3. Search

(a) *Preliminary considerations*:- The searching troops should be employed during daylight only. Before deciding on the best method of tackling the problem the officer commanding searching troops should take into account the civilian considerations in addition to the tactical ones. For example, markets or other places affecting the normal life of the city should be cleared as soon as feasible. Action to be taken where convents, church services, bonded warehouses and such like are included within the cordon requires previous consideration.

(b) *Number and distribution of troops*:- The number of searching troops required must depend on the type and congestion of houses in the area. An area 1 mile by 1 1/4 miles, chiefly composed of a maze of poor-class houses and narrow streets, was searched by 300 troops in 12 hours.

Searching troops should be organised into sections of one officer and thirteen other ranks prepared to work in two groups, one under the officer and one under a reliable NCO. In addition, the officer commanding searching troops should retain in reserve about one platoon (one officer and 20 other ranks), and if available, tanks and an armoured car.

(c) *Procedure*:- One block of buildings (size according to troops available) should be selected, and the whole force concentrated in cleaning it. Before search commences, observation posts should be established throughout the area to watch general movement, and local observation posts be posted on the roofs of the block being searched to watch for movement within the block.

The block concerned should be cordoned off and look-outs also be posted to watch the areas and gardens that cannot be observed from the roofs.

It will take time to arrange the above look outs in each block, but no search should be commenced until they are efficiently posted.

Meanwhile, all the male adults will be ordered to parade outside and in front of their own doorstep or at a prearranged point (*see* sub-para (d) below). The search will then commence. In the case of small houses, one officer, or selected NCO, with six men, should be allotted to each house. The whole block will be searched simultaneously, unless the number of troops is insufficient, in which case the search will commence from the outer ends simultaneously.

When a block has been searched, the local cordon troops, on advice from the officer commanding searchers, will move inwards and establish the cordon so as to exclude that block from the enclosed area. The local look outs concerned will not be removed until the cordon has been re-established.

Houses will be searched from the cellar upwards. Attention must be given to outhouses, cupboards, stables, lavatories, trap-doors, and receptacles likely to contain a man in cases where the quarry is individuals.

The reserve can frequently be used with advantage for sudden raids on selected places elsewhere in the cordoned area without interfering with the general plan of raiding by blocks.

(d) *Special Personnel*:- Special Intelligence personnel for identification will act under their own Commander under the orders of the officer commanding searching troops. They will move along and inspect the civilians' parades outside the houses. In addition, one selected specialist will be attached to the officer commanding searchers and each officer in charge of a number of Sections (variable). The specialists will not be put in command of troops.

(e) *Damage*:- In many cases doors must be forced owing to absence of owners (a beam propelled by a tank or motor vehicle is an economical method of forcing a lock). A special party equipped with hammers and nails will be detailed to nail up doors that have been forced after the house has been searched. Civil police should be called on to patrol such houses after the cordon has passed, to prevent looting.

Skeleton keys are useful as avoiding damage to doors. In all cases of damage a record will be kept by the officer commanding Section stating extent of damage and address. These reports will be collected by an officer detailed as Claims officer, who will further check and investigate damages as the searchers progress.

4. Co-operation.

Officers commanding cordon and searching troops will maintain close touch with each other throughout. The headquarters of searching troops must be in the vicinity of searchers, and will probably thus be distinct from cordon headquarters at the initial stages. A field telephone must therefore connect the two headquarters throughout. Close co-operation is also necessary with the civil police.

5. Headquarters Staff

Cordon Troops:- Commanding Officer, Staff Officer, Permit Officer (at an examining post), Orderly Officer, Specialist Officer, Medical Officer, and Claims Officer.

One motor car and ambulance.

Searching Troops:- Commanding Officer, Staff Officer, Permit Officer (at an examining post), Orderly Officer, Specialist Officer, Medical Officer, and Claims Officer.

One motor car and ambulance.

Also each headquarters requires a clerk, signallers, and DRs.

6. Precautions

(a) To prevent 'wanted' persons escaping under the disguise of an officer, soldier, or policeman, all officers, specialists and police must carry a pass or equivalent for identification purposes. Soldiers not recognised will be retained until identified; orderlies must therefore carry some means of identification.

(b) It is essential that all ranks fully understand that *no one, for any reason whatever*, is permitted to pass through the cordon except through an examining post.

APPENDIX VI

Escorts Travelling on Trains

IN VIEW OF the recent attacks on escorts and military parties travelling on the railways, the following instructions are forwarded for compliance by all such parties proceeding. No officer or NCO in command of a party is to proceed without knowledge of these instructions.

1. Officer commanding escort or party proceeding will, with the assistance of RTOs, select such carriages as he may deem most efficacious for the safety of the 'stores' that are being escorted and the escort. The officer commanding himself will select a central position, whence he can keep close touch with his party.

2. At the first halt the entire escort will change compartments, and if the journey is a lengthy one, will again move its position at a subsequent halt, with a view to concealing its dispositions

3. To prevent 'bunching', not more than one NCO and six men will travel in a compartment. No civilians will be permitted to share it. The removal of civilians from a compartment must be done with politeness.

4. In each compartment two men will be detailed as sentries to keep a look out from each side of the compartment, and protect the occupants against surprise from within or from outside. These men will have their rifles in their hands with a round in the chamber. The remainder of the party will have their rifles and ammunition ready for immediate use, and each man will know what to do in case of alarm. The construction of railway carriages varies, in some cases the corridor is in the centre, and the partition between compartments does not reach the roof, hence the importance of guarding against surprise from within.

5. No escort of less than one officer and 10 other ranks will proceed, the actual strength varying according to the duty being performed.

6. Prior to departure officer commanding escorts or parties will acquaint all ranks with his plan of counter-attack should the necessity arise, and it is suggested that such counter-attack, whenever the situation allows, will take the form of a sortie from the train against the attackers, but this must depend on circumstances, as in some cases an attempt to leave the compartments might be suicidal.

7. All officers travelling in plain clothes will make themselves known to escorts or parties proceeding, and will place themselves at the disposal of the officer commanding in the event of attack by rebels.

APPENDIX VII

26 June 1921
Troops' Action for Protection of Routes in City

1. Troops in Dublin must be prepared to take the following action for the protection of routes in the city:-

    (a) Piquet commanding points, such as roofs;

    (b) Patrol adjacent parallel routes.

The object of these arrangements is *primarily* to surprise the rebels should they endeavour to commit outrages in the vicinity.

2. The role of the piquets on commanding points is primarily to surprise and neutralise the rebels, who may wish to occupy similar points. In many cases the target offered by the rebels in the streets to such military piquets will not be favourable, chiefly on account of the presence of inoffensive civilians. Therefore, rebels on or adjacent to the ground level should normally be dealt with by the local Crown forces' escort and the flanking patrols.

3. The following precautions must be taken with regard to piqueting commanding points:-

(a) Previous reconnaissance when possible

(b) Troops should not enter a house with the obvious intention of piqueting the roof. Various methods can be used for concealing such intention. Every endeavour must be made to conceal the presence of the piquet. No more men than essential should be exposed, the remainder being kept under cover, where they can rest, but in close touch with the sentries. A room at the top of the house would frequently serve the purpose. To avoid leakage of information, it will generally be necessary to prevent the occupants of a piqueted house from leaving the building, or using the telephone, so long as the troops remain.

(c) The piquet must be prepared to meet an attack in the form of sniping or otherwise, from the flanks, front, rear, and from below. Bunching will be fatal to concealment and safety. The presence of the piquets must, as far as possible, be concealed if there is to be any hope of taking the rebels by surprise, which is so essential.

(d) Each piquet must know the approximate position of neighbouring piquets and of the flanking patrols.

(e) Where piquets have been in position for several hours, the rebels may have had time to detect them and prepare an ambush for them during withdrawal. The evacuation of the roof and building, and the move to barracks, must be carried out with caution, steps being taken throughout to guard against hostile attack.

(f) When necessary to piquet the same area frequently, the same position must not be taken up consecutively.

Positions must be varied as much as possible.

[Document date] 5 July 1921
Special Instructions to Battalions Marching Through Dublin
1. As soon as possible after disembarkation covering parties will be put out.
2. Battalions should march to barracks protected by an advanced and rear guard, which should consist of about 20 men in groups of three.
3. The packs of about 25 per cent of the men should be carried in the lorries to allow for greater freedom of action in case of attacks.
4. Sentries should have their rifles fully loaded. All men should have five rounds in the magazine. A proportion of Lewis guns should be ready for immediate action.
5. Intervals of at least 30 yards should be maintained between platoons.

APPENDIX VIII

Employment of Aeroplanes in Dublin District
5 March 1921 [Document date]

1. The RAF are prepared to co-operate as follows:-
   - (a) Escort to convoys
   - (b) Reconnaissance duties
   - (c) Raids, where rebels are likely to break into open country
   - (d) Attack and defence with machine guns (if carried)

Escort to Convoys

2. The following information will be required by the RAF:-
   - (a) Number (not type) of vehicles, and their distribution into advanced, main body, and rear party and flanking parties (if any)
   - (b) Route and destination
   - (c) Time the convoy will leave, and, in the case of a convoy leaving Dublin, the time it will clear the city, and approximate time of arrival at destination

In this case the action of the aeroplane would be to reconnoitre the route, report suspicions of an ambush, and assist the convoy in case of attack.

Note.- It may be assumed that one aeroplane can remain in the air for four hours (average).

Rreconnaissance

3. The observer in an aeroplane may be expected to detect:-

    (a) Road block of felled trees or wall

    (b) Broken-down bridge, or bridge with road surface destroyed if not camouflaged

    (c) Soldiers in khaki from persons in civilian clothing, but police are difficult to distinguish from latter

Communications

4. (a) Troops and police co-operating with aeroplane will carry:-

    (i) Verey pistols and red Verey lights as an SOS signal. (Also to be carried in aeroplanes.)

    (ii) A large-size signalling flag (white, with a blue band) to denote position of Commanding Officer. It will be waved horizontally, or placed flat on suitable ground.

(b) Messages will be dropped from the aeroplane at the above place (4 (a) (ii). But in the case of a moving column, the aeroplane will drop message in front of the column. When an aeroplane flies low and circles, it may be assumed that a message is about to be dropped.

(c) For operations of importance a wireless telephone set will probably be available for use between the OC troops and the aeroplane.

5. Before a combined operation (other than convoy duty), the pilot and OC troops must personally confer. Instructions to the pilot must be simple and definite. The area, route and place

to be reconnoitred and the position of the dropping ground will be clearly stated.

3 July 1921 [Document date]
Action When Aeroplane and Troop Train are Co-operating
Whenever an aeroplane is ordered to escort a troop train the following procedure will be observed:-

1. The aeroplane will not be sent up until the train has started, or is known to be starting, within half an hour at the utmost.
2. To ensure this the RTO will ring up the General Staff, Dublin District, as soon as he is certain what time the train will start, and the RAF squadron will be asked to function as soon as it is necessary to fly. Every effort must be made to ensure that the train keeps to time.
3. Intercommunication between the train and aeroplane will be by means of Verey lights.

To ensure that the aeroplane is kept under observation by the train the whole time, an officer with Verey pistol and the necessary cartridges will travel in the cab of the engine.

As an additional safeguard, officer commanding troop train will arrange that the Verey light signals can be fired from an alternative position in the train in case the officer on the engine is unable to see the aeroplane signals or to fire his Verey pistol.
4. The various signals to be used will be as follows:-
    (a) Initial communication, at the commencement of the journey, will be established by the firing of a green Verey light from the train, which will be answered similarly by the aeroplane. This procedure will be repeated if and

when a relieving aeroplane takes over escort.

(b) In the event of the aeroplane locating an ambush or damage to the line or wishing to stop the train for any reason, the pilot will fire red Verey lights.

(c) This signal will be acknowledged by the officer on the engine firing a green Verey light.

(d) If the ambush is located the plane will then fire a red Verey light over the ambushing party after stopping the train.

(e) When the train has stopped the aeroplane will drop a message on the train giving any information obtained.

(f) If the train runs into an ambush or obstruction without warning from the aeroplane, the officer on the engine will fire red Verey lights until acknowledged by the aeroplane by a green light.

(g) If assistance is required the aeroplane will drop a message giving all the information available at the nearest detachments.

5. Whenever a troop train stops for emergency reasons protecting piquets will be sent out to occupy commanding positions, and strong patrols will be pushed out towards the danger point. These parties must be detailed before the train starts and be suitably accommodated.

6. If any smoke or fire signals are observed the train should stop and investigations be made. If nothing is discovered the train will proceed with caution.

7. When more than one train is required to carry a unit, the trains will move as close to one another as possible, each train preceded by a pilot engine, in the same block.

Each troop train will carry two Verey pistols and a supply of the necessary cartridges.

Appendix IX

Subject: Passes

12 June 1921 [Document date]
In Dublin District:-
Forces of the Crown

1. No member of any forces of the Crown will be permitted to enter a place occupied by armed troops unless either-

    (a) In possession of a photograph pass stamped partially on the photograph and signed by the DPM, GHQ, APM, Dublin District; or the Castle Commandant;

    (b) Identified at the entrance as a *known* member of the unit holding the place concerned, or a *known* member of any other unit or formation of Dublin District.

2. (a) A member of the forces of the Crown not included in the above categories will be detained at the entrance until authority is obtained for his admittance from the OC place concerned.

    (b) Forces of the Crown proceeding on duty to any place held by troops should be in possession of orders stamped with their own headquarters' stamp, which, when necessary, can be offered as an explanation for requiring to enter the place.

Such orders will on no account be considered as a pass, but be forwarded to the OC, the place concerned for his information. No more persons of such parties will be permitted to enter than are absolutely necessary to carry out the duty concerned.

Civilians

3. (a) There are only three types of civilian passes that will be accepted in Dublin District area, and all are photograph passes, namely:-

Pass for civilians living in barracks

Pass for civilians living out of barracks

Special RASC civilian pass for admittance to Royal Barracks only

No more civilian passes should be issued than absolutely necessary, and each one will include the name of the barracks at which they are eligible, and will not be accepted at any other barracks. In isolated cases a pass will be issued for admittance to any barracks in Dublin District area, but this will only be done provided that the Officer Commanding each barracks concerned has previously given his approval to the APM.

(b) From 23 June inclusive no civilian male or female (including girls and boys) will be admitted to a place held by armed troops unless either:-

(i) The person can be identified at the gate as being a regular employee in the place concerned. This identification is only to be done by a responsible representative of the OC barracks concerned, who is *known* to the Guard Commander and in touch with the names of dismissed employees;

or

(ii) The person can produce a photograph pass stamped partially on the photograph and signed by one of the following:-

APM, Dublin

DPM, GHQ

Castle Commandant (for admittance to the Castle)

OC, RASC (for admittance to Royal Barracks, by south-west gate only).

(c) Casual civilians will be detained at the entrance, and only be permitted to enter by order of the Officer Commanding the place concerned, who will satisfy himself as to their *bona fides*. He will also ensure that, when admitted, they are not permitted to move about without supervision, and that they depart as soon as their business is completed.

Sentry on the Gate
READ THIS:

1. The rebels possess military and police uniforms and vehicles of all kinds, and will try to get into your barracks disguised in these uniforms. They will probably drive up in a stolen lorry or armoured car dressed as soldiers, or in a stolen military touring car dressed as officers, and expect you to open the gate. When you have once opened the gate they may have you at their mercy. They may try to slip in dressed as soldiers, as if in company with real soldiers.

2. BE ON YOUR GUARD, AND SUSPECT everyone that you do not know, whether military, police, civilian male,

female or child; also every kind of vehicle, whether ARMOURED CAR, touring car, Ford car, lorry, cart, military or civilian, must be treated with suspicion.

3. If you do not know a person or a party in a vehicle, do not open the gate. Keep them outside until a photographic pass in produced like one of the three attached. Make sure that the photograph is like the person. If no photographic pass is produced, and the person cannot be identified by you, ask for instructions from your Commander BEFORE OPENING THE GATE.

4. You are in charge of the gate, and can keep outside anyone that you do not know or suspect, whatever his rank may be. No pass except one of the three attached will be accepted by you.

8 June 1921 [Document date]

APPENDIX X

As Affects Dublin District During Period June 1920 to July 1921

(A) Strength of the Opposing Forces
Military

1920 January to April	9,610	All ranks
1920 April to December	8,965	All ranks
December to July, 1921	10,084	All ranks

Auxiliaries (RIC) approximately	400	All ranks
RIC	1,200	All ranks

(Excluding Depot and Training Camp.)

IRA - The following strength of the IRA is estimated from information gathered previous to the Truce, and from information as to new units formed since the Truce, and from the laid down establishment of the IRA. It is probable that a number of new companies have been formed, of which no details have been obtained. This is especially so in the 7th Dublin Battalion. This area has recruited largely since the Truce, and the estimate for the 6th and 7th Battalions is very low. The estimate for officers is probably nearly accurate, but in regard to other ranks the estimate is a minimum.

In the event of a renewal of hostilities it is thought that in some areas many members of the IRA who now parade will not fight till forced to by their comrades. This is especially so in Meath, and the Fingal and Wicklow brigades.

It is not possible to estimate the number of arms in possession of units. During peace training it is thought that only IR police and officers of the IRA are in possession of arms. A certain number are kept in training camps for instruction, but the main portion are kept in company and battalion dumps.

It is estimated that the IRA, on the renewal of hostilities, will be in a position to arm as follows:-

Rifles	10 per cent
Revolvers	25 per cent
Shot guns	30 per cent
Bombers	35 per cent

(5 per cent per company are specially trained bombers).

The number of machine guns imported since the Truce is unknown, but *An t'Oglac* states that it is proposed to arm each company with a machine gun. Although rumours that each company has a gun are prevalent, few have been seen, but one gun per battalion is a minimum estimate.

The Cumann na mBan and Fianna, both of which are armed to a certain extent with revolvers, are used for the most part for scouting and despatch carrying. The Fianna may be expected to carry out any operations such as undertaken by the IRA. The strength of the Fianna may be estimated as half that of the IRA.

As Affects Dublin District During Period June 1920 to July 1921

Estimated Strength of the IRA

	Officers	Other Ranks
Dublin brigade (including Kingstown area) (7 battalions)	201	4,160
Wicklow brigade (3 battalions)	66	650
Fingal brigade (3 battalions)	72	750
Meath brigade (6 battalions)	195	2,350
No. 1 brigade (N. Louth) (probably 3 battalions)	123	600
No. 9 brigade (S. Louth) (probably 2 battalions)	96	480
Cavan brigade, IRA (8 battalions)	353	1,960
Monaghan brigade (5 battalions)	267	1,500
Total	1,373	12,450

The above estimate must be taken as a minimum.

Editor's note: The Dublin, Wicklow, Fingal, Meath, and south Louth brigades are assigned by the British to 1st Eastern Division. The North Louth brigade is assigned to 4th Northern Division, while the Monaghan brigade is assigned to 5th Northern Division. The Army was unsure if the Cavan brigade was assigned to the 5th or 6th Northern Division.

(B) Military Material Lost Through Known Rebel Action

Motor lorries	5
Crossley tenders	6
Motor cycles	1
Cycles	13
Touring cars	2
Motor ambulances	2
Ford van	1
Hotchkiss guns	2
Lewis guns	2
Revolvers and pistols	13
Rifles	16
Horses	1 killed
	1 wounded
Mules	3 killed
	1 wounded
Military stores (truck loads of timber for R.E.) (destroyed)	3
(wagon loads) (destroyed)	3
Telephones, portable	7
Telephone apparatus (hand carts containing 5 sets)	2
Huts (destroyed at Arklow)	5

Shell Factory. MT repairing shops and ordnance stores (partially destroyed)

Rebel Material Lost

Revolvers and pistols	424
Rifles	95
Shot guns	112
Swords and bayonets	89
Bombs or hand grenades	960
Hand-grenade cases	150
Detonators	10,237
Rifle and revolver ammunition	30,192 rounds
Sporting cartridges	1,593
Rifle grenades	10
Shells, 18-pdr.	6
Shells, German 7.7	2
Motor cars	7
Motor cycles (2 with side cars)	11
Cycles	24
Lewis gun	1
Machine gun, German	1
Casting for Stokes mortar	1

Quantities of explosives, including:- Sticks of gelignite; sticks of dynamite; boxes of ammonite; boxes of cordite; bags of gunpowder; coils of fuse (various); percussion tubes; land mines.

(C) Arrests, and Disposal

Arrested	3,170
Interned	1,283
Convicted	182
Hanged	6

Killed attempting to escape   2
Released   1,697

(D) Casualties of Opposing Forces
Military
    Officers
        Killed   13
        Wounded   9
        Died of wounds   1

    Other Ranks
        Killed   9
        Wounded   59
        Died of wounds   2

Rebels
(Definitely known, but the true figure is considerably larger)
        Killed   41
        Wounded   70

APPENDIX XI

Subject: Patrolling in the City

THE FOLLOWING SUGGESTIONS are issued as a guide to patrol work in towns in aid to the civil power.

1. Abandon all fixed beats.

2. Each battalion should divide its part of the city into patrol areas.

3. The objective is to gain control of the streets and break up resistance.

4. Examine each sector in the light of local circumstances and calculate the form and extent of likely resistance, then dispose forces accordingly.

5. In some parts patrols of eight or ten fully armed men will suffice. In others it may be necessary to employ up to the strength of a platoon. Patrols should not move in mass, but should work in groups, and in the case of strong patrols scouts should be used to watch the front, rear and flanks.

6. Where police are co-operating a preliminary conference between the officer in charge of the patrol and of the police concerned should be carried out.

7. As the situation develops the concentration of patrols in those parts where resistance continues should be considered.

8. Patrols should not remain out for fixed periods of time but should come back into barracks or billets for rest, so that the men may not be over-strained.

9. A strong line should be taken by searching persons, motor cars, other vehicles, and houses, so that it may become difficult for ill-disposed persons to carry arms.

10. Searching should be carried out by one or two men covered by the remainder. The searchers should carry out their work quietly and quickly. Altercations or arguments should be avoided.

11. Patrols should work in groups, moving on both sides of the street some distance apart, so as to avoid offering a concentrated target.

12. Loiterers, groups and collecting crowds should be promptly moved on or dispersed.

13. Patrols should frequently halt and take stock of the situation.

14. When fired on men should at once lie down and return the fire. All crowding together on the part of the patrol should be avoided.

15. As far as possible men on patrol should be lightly equipped and wear rubber soles, or the equivalent.

16. During the night halting near street lamps or other lights may prove fatal.

17. Foot patrols can be supported by motor lorry or motor car patrols; these should cover a wider beat, but keep in touch with foot patrols. At night the more mobile patrols can also search persons, motor cars and other vehicles.

18. All patrols should be prepared to lay in ambush.

19. In time of actual or expected disturbances, strong patrols

should at once take over control. The confinement of troops and police to barracks on such occasions is damaging the moral of men and discouraging to loyal elements.

20. When there is excitement owing to the assembly of large numbers of persons, the patrols of police and troops should be sent out on strength to assert the law. They should see that motor cars are complying with the motor regulations, search cars and strongly suppress any disorder.

21. Searching of motor cars should be thorough; the hood, seats, cushions, tool box, spare wheels and bonnet should be carefully examined. Cases have occurred where revolvers and ammunition were found in the horsehair of cushions.

22. Houses of suspicion should receive continual attention especially by night. Such action is disconcerting to the inmates concerned.

23. When order has been restored patrols should not slacken. All breaches of ordinary law should be dealt with so that the public may realise that order has been restored.

APPENDIX XII

Protection Against Surprise

I WISH AGAIN to impress on all commanders of whatever rank the utmost importance of constantly instructing their officers, NCOs, and men in the methods the rebels adopt to outwit us, and thereby murder officers and other ranks when off their guard, effect the release of prisoners and obtain their successes.

One point requiring the closest attention is the necessity for us never to allow ourselves to be lulled into a sense of false security, but at all times and under all conditions to be on the alert and suspicious of danger.

One of the rebels' strongest weapons is the possession of military and police uniforms. He has used them sparingly so far, but I have not the slightest doubt that one day he will make use of them on a large scale and at many places simultaneously. If we are not prepared for this we shall suffer severe reverses.

It must be a rigid order that no officer is allowed into any barrack or quarters unless he produces his authorised pass, with photo (except in cases of officers being thoroughly well known personally).

Armed men or armoured cars will not be allowed to enter under any circumstances, until their identity had been thoroughly established. It is better to keep a party of our own men waiting half an hour than to run the risk of letting in armed rebels.

Such explanations as 'I am an officer', or 'We are a party of the .... shires', will not be accepted by a sentry.

These precautions are specially necessary in small barracks and with detached guards, also in any place where there are prisoners or internees.

It is to be remembered that every person in this country in mufti, man or women, is a potential enemy, but while insisting on all ranks behaving with the ordinary courtesy due to their profession, we must insist on everything being done to prevent men getting on too friendly or intimate terms will civilians, as this is a source by which the enemy gain information, though done in such a way that the giver of the information does not realise it.

It is not sufficient to issue one order on this matter. All commanders will make a constant practise of lecturing those under them on the subject. No week should pass without the battalion, battery, company and platoon commanders talking to their men on the subject, otherwise it becomes a dead letter.

It is only constant instruction that will ensue constant vigilance and suspicion.

The rebels are hard pressed, and will stick at nothing, so let us be prepared.

Rebels found masquerading in military or police uniforms who are not actually killed in the course of the fight will be liable to be shot on conviction by military court.

APPENDIX XIII

Description of Dublin District Area

1920
The area originally consisted of the cities of Dublin and Drogheda, and Counties Dublin and Wicklow. The dividing line between 24th and 25th (P.) Brigades was the River Liffey, inclusive to former.

On 10 February 1920
Dunlavin RIC Division (Co. Wicklow) was handed to 5th Division.

On 25 June 1920
Co. Meath was included in the 24th Brigade Area – Drogheda remaining with that brigade.

On 24 June 1920
Counties Monaghan, Cavan and Louth were taken over by Dublin District. These counties including Drogheda – became the new 26th (P.) Brigade Area.

On 23 November 1921
Swanlinbar RIC division (Co. Cavan) was handed over to
5th division.

Formation Headquarters were as follows:-

Dublin District	Dublin Castle
24th (P.) Brigade	Royal Barracks, Dublin
25th (P.) Brigade	Kilmainham
	(later Richmond Barracks, Dublin)
26th (P.) Brigade	Dundalk

Editor's Appendices

APPENDIX A

The Development and Organisation of Intelligence in Dublin during 1920–1921

This appendix is an extract from the Record of the Rebellion in Ireland in 1920-21, Volume II: Intelligence.

(i) *Area and population*:- The situation in Dublin was so unique that it was worth considering it in some detail. The area of the city is approximately 8 square miles, and if the suburbs, including Kingstown, are included, the area of Greater Dublin is about 14 square miles. The population of the city is 230,000, and the inclusion of the suburbs adds about 170,000 to the above figure.

Throughout the period under consideration three GHQs existed in Dublin, namely – (1) the Headquarters of the Civil Government, including the office of the Chief of Police at the Castle; (2) the Military GHQ, at Parkgate, at the north-western end of the city, and (3) GHQ, IRA, which directed the Sinn Féin plans as best it could from various houses in and about Dublin.

The city is divided, roughly speaking, into two equal parts by the river Liffey which is crossed by numerous bridges. It is a maze of narrow streets and alleys set in no order. There is little definite residential area, slums and tenement houses are found everywhere, and in the older part of the city there are many ramifications of underground cellars in which men, munitions and munition factories can be hidden. There are innumerable small shops and comparatively few large stores. It is, in fact, an ideal town for guerrilla operations.

The inhabitants are of all classes and the city is densely populated. The traders, although opposed to British rule and supporters of Sinn Féin, were openly friendly to the Crown Forces. Shop assistants and factory workers formed the backbone of the IRA.

All classes are permeated with mistrust and suspicion owing to the mixture of religions and politics. A considerable minority were professedly loyal but were so intimidated that they refused to give information even when they themselves had been the sufferers by IRA action.

(ii) *The organisation and strength of IRA formations and units in and about Dublin:*- As was expected in the largest city in Ireland and the area in which the GHQ, IRA, was situated, the organisation of the IRA units was the most complete and their relative strength greater than in any other area of the same size.

These formation and units were as follows:-

(a) *Dublin city and Dublin county, south of Dublin city.*

One Brigade consisting of four City Battalions and one 'South County' Battalion (6th). Also a 5th Battalion of which little is known. This unit was probably used as 'GHQ Troops' for the defence of the GHQ in Dublin. Total units – 6 battalions consisting of 52 companies. Strength - Approximately 201 officers, 4160 other ranks.

(b) *Fingal, i.e., Co. Dublin north of Dublin city*

One Brigade consisting of 3 Battalions or 15 companies. Strength – approximately 72 officers and 750 other ranks.

(c) *Co. Wicklow*

One brigade consisting of 3 battalions or 13 companies. Strength – approximately 66 officers and 650 ranks.

Total unit strength: Three Brigades consisting of 12 battalions or 80 companies.

Total approximate strength in personnel: 339 officers and 5,560 other ranks.

In addition to the above the '*Fianna Éireann*' or Boy Scouts and '*Cumann na mBan*' or Women's Organisation formed auxiliary units for intelligence and communication. The latter also carried out medical duties for the IRA such as first aid and nursing.

Organisation of GHQ:- The fact that the GHQ of the IRA existed in Dublin affected to a considerable degree the efficiency of the local formations and units. There is reason to believe and it is natural to suppose that the Dublin Brigade was much more under the influence of GHQ than any other unit, and that some of the officers on the staff at GHQ were also executive officers in the Dublin Brigade. Ambushes and bombing attacks on the Crown Forces were more numerous in Dublin than in other cities, and to a great extent this was due to the influence of their GHQ. Captured documents show that reports on such rebel action were systematically forwarded by the Dublin Brigade to GHQ, who criticised the conduct of operations, and thus exercised a close personnel supervision.

As far as can be ascertained the organisation of the GHQ was as follows:-

The Commander in Chief was a purely nominal position held by the President of the Republic. When de Valera was in America, Arthur Griffith was President and it is possible that Michael Collins then became Commander in Chief as Arthur Griffith had never identified himself with the military section of Sinn Féin. When Arthur Griffith was arrested, Michael Collins became Acting-President, and therefore titular as well as actual Commander in Chief, and it was probably during this period that he gained that

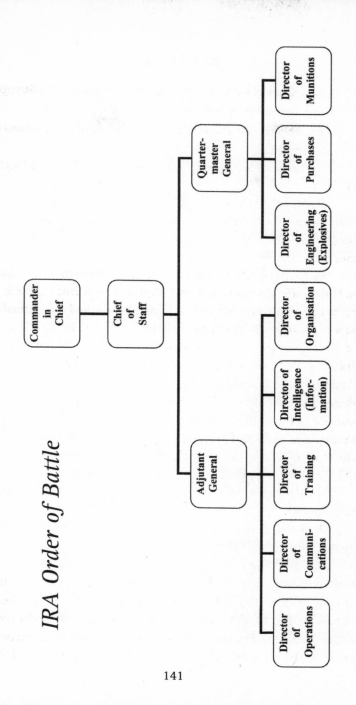

IRA Order of Battle

ascendancy which caused him subsequently to be looked on as Commander in Chief by the rank and file.

The relative position of the President, the Commander in Chief and the Minister of Defence have never been defined clearly.

It has been almost impossible to obtain definite evidence of the actual organisation of sub-sections of the staff of GHQ, IRA and the table is an approximation from the scraps of information obtained from time to time. Owing to incessant raids the leaders found it too dangerous to maintain properly organised offices and their staff work was in consequence somewhat primitive. For example, their Order of Battle (considerably out of date) was contained in a small pocket book carried about personally by the Chief of Staff, and the Provisional Government in February 1922, was ignorant as to which units comprised the 2nd Southern Division.

(iii) *The Crown Forces*:- As regards the organisation and disposition of the Crown Forces, one infantry brigade was quartered and operated north of the Liffey and the other south of the river. Each had its own brigade and battalion intelligence officers, and the co-operation of intelligence and operations in the two areas of the city depended on the staff of Dublin District, which included an area considerably larger than Greater Dublin, and which, in July 1921, consisted of the counties, Cavan, Monaghan, Louth, Meath, Dublin and Wicklow.

There was a Divisional Commissioner, RIC, in Dublin. His local centre was, however, in Dundalk, and dealt with intelligence questions connected with the counties of Louth, Monaghan, and Cavan only. Executive police operations in Dublin City were controlled to a very large extent by the Chief of Police, in conjunction, of course, with the GOC, Dublin District, both of whom had their office in the Castle.

(iv) *Intelligence in Dublin*:- Up to the summer of 1919, the military relied for their intelligence almost entirely on the DMP in the city, and on the RIC in the country, but these sources were practically closed about the end of 1919 by the murder campaign. At the beginning of 1920 the military intelligence staff consisted of a junior officer, attached to the 'G' staff, whose scope of activities was very limited as he had no organised means of obtaining information. There was no battalion intelligence officers at this time, but some regimental officers, who interested themselves in the Sinn Féin movement during the summer of 1919, had got in touch with the IRA. This showed the possibilities of an organised military intelligence service for Dublin District and a specially selected officer took charge of this branch on 1 March 1920. He got in touch with various civil sources of information and achieved a fair degree of success in spite of the fact that he was hampered by want of funds.

In April it was decided still further to expand and reorganise this intelligence branch, to form a plain clothes branch, and to collect both military and political information. In May a GSO (1) was selected to take charge of it.

A school of instruction for suitable agents was formed in England. There they received practical and theoretical instruction on the duties they would have to carry out in Ireland. Agents were sent over in various capacities for which they were chosen according to their abilities and qualifications.

Dublin District was in the first instance divided into six areas each in charge of a head agent who controlled his agents and obtained information by such means as he was able to devise. By the end of September 1920, the system was extended from Drogheda to Arklow and much useful information was obtained not only about this area but about Sinn Féin in England and about Irish secret societies in the USA.

In 1921 nearly all the officers of the Dublin Brigade, IRA, were known, and a good percentage of them had been arrested, including the IRA Director of Intelligence, the head of their secret service and four battalion IOs. There were trained agents on most of the boats coming to Dublin and Kingstown. Eight of the principal departments of Dáil Éireann and the IRA had been raided successfully and three dumps had been taken. Twice was the GHQ of the IRA raided, on one occasion the Chief of Staff's personal office and plans being captured and only three days before the Truce the office of the IRA police was taken.

Up to the end of 1920 this organisation, known as the Special Branch, Dublin District, worked directly under the military authorities and the co-operation between 'intelligence' and operations was most successful. The brigade intelligence officers were in close touch and themselves opened up some very good channels and battalion intelligence officers, who were appointed early in 1920, though their sources of information were limited, also achieved some good results.

The murders of 21 November 1920 temporarily paralysed the special branch. Several of its most efficient members were murdered and the majority of the others resident in the city were brought into the Castle and Central Hotel for safety. This centralisation in the most inconvenient places possible greatly decreased the opportunities for obtaining information and for re-establishing anything in the nature of a secret service.

Early in 1921, the Special Branch with its records, were handed over to the Chief of Police and amalgamated with Police Intelligence, which had already had a service of secret agents directed from London. The Director of Police Intelligence was thus responsible for the organisation, henceforward know as the 'D' branch, which had become partly intelligence and partly executive, and the Central Intelligence Office usurped functions which were properly those of a Local Centre, Dublin, which was never created.

This transfer of what was in fact the military intelligence system was a grave mistake. For personal reasons it was wholly unpopular among the personnel of the Special Branch, and unfortunately personal considerations can rarely be left out of account in questions connected with secret service. The organisation continued to work for the army but was responsible to a new master, the Chief of Police, consequently the driving power behind the agents gradually diminished. The GOC, Dublin District, remained responsible for intelligence in an area where he had not a sufficient organisation and ceased to control the agents working in his command. Consequently duplicate organisations both to check the police information and to act as a liaison became necessary. The result was delay in taking action, overlapping in work and a registry created on the lines of compromise and satisfactory to neither military or police.

The duties for which the various branches concerned were responsible were as under:-

(i) *'D' Branch, Chief of Police*:- Responsible for collating intelligence referring to Dublin District from:-

    (a) Secret Agents' reports.

    (b) Military Intelligence reports.

    (c) Informers' reports both from its own and military informers.

    (d) Documents captured by members of 'D' Branch and by military and police on raids.

    (e) RIC and DMP reports on the area.

    (f) Scotland House reports referring to the area.

    (g) Passing information to Registry, Chief of Police, for filing.

Responsible for passing the collated information to the General Staff, Dublin District, for action.

(ii) *Gen. Staff, Intelligence, Dublin District*:- Responsible for keeping the GOC informed of all organisation, future activities, methods and intentions of the IRA and its members by:-

(a) Organisation and efficient working of Brigade and Unit Intelligence Organisations.

(b) Distribution of intelligence from 'D' Branch to Brigades and Units affected.

(c) Collection and collation of intelligence from military sources, informers, prisoners, etc., and distributing such information to 'D' Branch, GHQ, and such military units as are affected.

(d) Advising the GOC on and making out charges for the recommendation for internment of such prisoners as could not be tried by Court-Martial.

(e) Enquiring into characters of civilians employed by the military.

(f) Internal Intelligence in units of the Dublin District.

(g) Keeping the Order of Battle and Army List of the IRA.

(iii) *Raid Bureau, Chief of Police*:- Responsible for:-

(a) Filing all reports on raids.

(b) Receiving all documents, arms and articles seized in such raids by both the military and police. Filing and safeguarding them so that at a future date they may be used as evidence against the owner if arrested.

(c) Epitomising such documents and distributing the epitomes to all concerned.

(iv) *Registry, Chief of Police*:- Registering all information and keeping the personal files and personal cards of all suspects. This registry was for the joint use of all branches of the Chief of Police, and for reference by General Staff, Intelligence, Dublin District.

The Special, or 'D' Branch, was a peculiar organisation, as secret service organisations generally are. It was built up in the first instance by enthusiastic amateurs who neither knew nor cared about the distinctions between I. (a) and I. (b). It was partly pure intelligence and partly executive. It had its own 'constitution' and in the event of its official head taking action to which the original creators objected, they did not hesitate to raise their objections in unmistakable fashion. Persons accustomed to police or detective work, where objections are usually limited and definite, might and did regard the personnel as amateurs. It is questionable, however, whether, if some obvious faults of organisation had been rectified, this branch would not have been as good and efficient as was possible in the peculiar circumstances that obtained and whether if it had been wisely handled it might not have been extended to throughout Ireland with good results.

That intelligence as a whole obtained good results in Dublin was due mainly to personnel effort rather than to good organisation. The circumstances were peculiar and the fact that both the Director of Police Intelligence and the GOC, Dublin District, had their offices in the Castle, was likely to make the former see Dublin out of all proportion and to act in some respects as a local centre, in others as a county inspector rather than in his proper capacity.

If all intelligence and all operations in the city had been controlled from one office better results might have been achieved and a great deal of friction and irritation would certainly have been avoided.

Appendix B

Biographies of Senior British Officers, Dublin District

Major General Gerald Farrell Boyd
General Officer Commanding, Dublin District

Boyd was born on 17 October 1877, and so was in his early forties when he commanded the Dublin District during the War of Independence. Prior to being commissioned, he served in the ranks for over four years. Boyd was commissioned into the East Yorkshire Regiment as a 2nd Lieutenant on 5 May 1900, and promoted lieutenant in the same regiment on 26 April 1902. On 19 March 1904, he transferred to Leinster Regiment, and was to gain promotion to major on a transfer to the Royal Irish Regiment on 18 March 1915.

He was to hold a variety of posts in World War One, prior to the outbreak of the war; he served as the brigade major of the 11th Infantry Brigade of the Eastern Command. This brigade was assigned to the British Expeditionary Force on 5 August 1914, and Boyd would serve with it until 23 February 1915. From 3 March 1915, until 15 July 1918, he would serve in a number of staff roles, as a GSO Grade 2 with the 1st Division, BEF, as a GSO Grade 1 with 6th Division, BEF, and finally as brigadier general on the General Staff, 5th Army Corps of the British Armies in France. On 16 July, 1918, he became brigade commander of the 170th infantry brigade, and was promoted to divisional commander, 46th Division on 5 September 1918, a position he held until 23 March 1919. From 24 March 1919 to 6 October 1919, he served in the British Army of the Rhine, as a brigade commander and divisional commander with the Mid Division, and as brigadier general on the general staff of the BAOR. On 31 December 1919, he was appointed general officer commanding, Dublin District.

His military awards included, the CB, CMG, DSO, and DCM. He was also the honorary colonel of the Leinster Regiment.

The 24th Provisional Brigade

Colonel Richard Deare Furley Oldman
Officer Commanding, 24th Provisional Brigade
Oldman was born on 17 June 1877, and commissioned into the Norfolk Regiment as a 2nd Lieutenant on 20 February 1897. He was promoted lieutenant on 19 April 1898, captain on 25 February 1905, and major on 25 April 1915.

He served with the West African Frontier Force from 14 February 1903 to 17 February 1908. On 14 September 1914, he was appointed a deputy assistant adjutant general to the GHQ of the BEF, a post he held until 12 March 1915, when he left to become a temporary lieutenant colonel in the Cheshire Regiment. He was promoted to temporary brigadier general on 15 April 1916, and given command of the 117th Infantry Brigade of the British Armies in France. His other brigade commands during the war were, Sheppey Infantry Brigade, Home Forces, 20 March 1917 to 2 November 1917, the 15th Infantry Brigade, British Armies in France, 3 November 1917 to 14 April 1919. On 15 April 1919, he returned to the rank of temporary lieutenant colonel in command of 53rd Battalion, Bedfordshire and Headfordshire Regiment, but on 1 August 1919, Oldman returned to brigade command, being given the 2nd Brigade, E Division, BAOR.

He was appointed Commander, 24th Provisional Brigade, on 10 August, 1920. He was serving in Dublin, already as battalion commander of 1st Battalion, Wiltshire Regiment.

His military awards include the CMG, and the DSO.

Lietuenant Colonel Robert Napier Bray
Officer Commanding, 2nd Battalion, The Duke of Wellington's Regiment
Bray was born on 7 December 1872, and was commissioned from the Militia into the West Riding Regiment as a 2nd Lieutenant on 12 December 1894. He was promoted lieutenant on 15 September 1897, captain on 28 February 1901, and major on 5 April 1911. He served as a battalion adjutant in the regiment from 29 January 1903 to 8 March 1906.

He served as an adjutant in the Indian Volunteers from 14 June 1906 to 13 April 1910. He was commandant, Shanghai Volunteers from 29 June 1913 to 24 May 1915. During World War One, he served mainly as a brigade commander, he commanded the 8th Infantry Brigade, from 7 December 1916 to 3 April 1917, the 171st Brigade, from 4 April 1917 to 22 September 1917, the 189th Brigade, from 5 January 1918 to 19 March 1918, and the 48th Infantry Brigade, from 20 June 1918 to 1 May 1919.

He was made a lieutenant colonel on 11 December 1918.

His military awards include the CMG, and the DSO.

Lieutenant Colonel Henry Arbuthnot Carr
Officer Commanding, 2nd Battalion The Worcestershire Regiment
Carr was born 2 September 1872. He was commissioned into the Worcestershire Regiment as a 2nd Lieutenant on 21 October 1893. He was promoted within the Worcestershire Regiment, was made lieutenant on 14 December 1896, captain on 17 February 1900, and

major on 11 June 1910. He served as battalion adjutant from 6
March 1903 to 5 September 1906.

He served as an assistant provost marshal in South Africa from
1 September 1900 until 26 June 1902. During World War One, he
served as a temporary or acting lieutenant colonel for both the 7th
Battalion, Royal Sussex Regiment and the 8th Battalion,
Worcestershire Regiment, from 5 August 1916 to 30 March 1919.
He was appointed a lieutenant colonel of the Worcestershire
Regiment on 2 March 1919.

Lieutenant Colonel Cyril De Putron
Officer Commanding, 1st Battalion, Lancashire Fusiliers

De Putron was born on 3 February 1874. He was commissioned into
the North Lancashire Regiment as a 2nd Lieutenant from the militia on 29 May 1895. He was promoted to lieutenant on 11 October
1896. On 15 June 1901, he transferred to the Lancashire Fusiliers
and was promoted captain. He served as a temporary major from
17 March 1915 to 31 August 1915, and was promoted major in the
Lancashire Fusiliers on 1 September 1915. He was appointed lieutenant colonel on 22 March 1920.

De Putron served as an instructor in the school of musketry
at Hythe from 1 April 1909 to 31 March 1913. This was not his only
involvement in military education he was commandant of the
school of instruction of the Egyptian Expeditionary Force from 11
October 1917 to 9 May 1918, and commandant of the School of
Musketry, Southern Command, 19 August 1918 to 11 March 1919.

During World War One, he was attached to the general staff of
both the Northern and Eastern Command from 1 December 1913 to 16
March 1915. He served as a GSO Grade 2 with the Mediterranean
Expeditionary Force from 17 March 1915 to 15 April 1916. He served
for various periods as the battalion commander of the 2/15 battalion, London Regiment, from 2 May 1916 to 11 March 1919.

Lieutenant Colonel Anthony Julian Reddie
Officer Commanding, 1st Battalion, South Wales Borderers

Reddie was born on 7 August 1873, and was commissioned into the South Wales Borderers as a 2nd Lieutenant on 19 November 1892. He was promoted within the regiment to lieutenant on 1 July 1895, to captain on 22 September 1901, and major on 9 June 1913. He served as adjutant in the regiment from 2 September 1901 to 1 September 1904. He served as a temporary lieutenant colonel of the South Wales Borderers from 1 December 1914 to 20 August 1915.

From 17 November 1909 to 16 March 1913, Reddie served as an adjutant in the Territorial Force. During World War One, he was a temporary brigadier general, commanding the 1st Infantry Brigade from 23 August 1915 to 9 November 1917, the Welsh Reserve Infantry Brigade, Home Forces, from 10 November 1917 to 2 April 1918, and the 187th Infantry Brigade, British Armies in France, from 2 April 1918 to 17 March 1919.

From 2 April 1919 to 18 August 1919, he was for periods, the acting or temporary lieutenant colonel of the 51st Battalion, South Wales Borderers. He was appointed lieutenant colonel on 6 December 1919.

His military awards include the CMG, and the DSO.

The 25th Provisional Brigade

Colonel Cranley Charlton Onslow
Officer Commanding, 25th Provisional Brigade

Onslow was born on 19 September 1869, and was commissioned as a 2nd lieutenant into the Bedfordshire Regiment on 9 November 1889, and promoted lieutenant on 11 August 1891. He was made a captain in the Bedfordshires on 1 July 1898, and a major on 8 June 1910.

He served as an adjutant in the Indian Volunteers from 2 May 1900 to 2 May 1905, and a officer commandant of gentleman cadets at the Royal Military College from 16 May 1910 to 21 July 1914.

During World War One, he served mainly as a brigade commander, and from 16 June 1916 until 31 March 1919, he was the officer commanding of the 57th Infantry Brigade, and the 7th Infantry Brigade, both of the British Armies in France, and of the 225th Infantry Brigade, home force.

He was appointed commander of the 25th Provisional Brigade on 20 April, 1920.

His military awards include the CMG, the CBE, and the DSO.

Lieutenant Colonel Hugh Roger Headlam
Officer Commanding, 1st Battalion, King's Own Regiment
Headlam was born on 15 July 1877, and commissioned into the Yorkshire and Lancashire Regiment as a 2nd Lieutenant on 8 September 1897. He was promoted within this regiment to lieutenant on 2 November 1899, to captain on 2 April 1903, and to major on 25 April 1915

He served as a staff officer in South Africa from 29 July 1901 to 15 July 1902, on intelligence and provost duties. From 12 March 1903 to 31 January 1913, he was employed with the Egyptian Army. From 5 August 1914 to 31 October 1914, he was a staff captain involved in landing the BEF in France. From 1 November 1914 to 19 February 1915, he served as a staff captain with 16th Infantry Brigade, and then as a brigade major with the 18th Infantry Brigade from 20 February 1915 to 31 August 1915. He was appointed a temporary brigadier general on 12 June 1916, and given command of 64th Infantry Brigade, an appointment he held until 15 August 1918. Holding the rank of brigadier general, he served as Inspector of Infantry from 16 August 1918 until October 1919. During this period, he also served as the acting or temporary lieutenant colonel of the 1/4 Battalion, Yorkshire and Lancashire Regiment from 14 April 1919 to 31 July 1919 and from 1 August 1919 to 19 August 1919. He also served as a GSO Grade 1 with GHQ India from 25 October 1919 to 30 May 1920.

He was appointed a lieutenant colonel of the Yorkshire and Lancashire Regiment on 3 May 1920.

Lieutenant Colonel Bryan Chetwynd-Stapylton
Officer Commanding, The Cheshire Regiment
Chetwynd-Stapylton was born on 10 June 1877, and commissioned as a 2nd Lieutenant into the Cheshires on 9 January 1892. He was promoted within the regiment to lieutenant on 15 May 1896, to captain on 15 December 1900, and to major on 2 August 1913. He was appointed lieutenant colonel in the Cheshire Regiment on 16 October 1919.

He served as an adjutant in the militia from 8 November 1903 to 7 November 1906. He served as a staff captain in the war office from 19 March 1910 to 31 March 1912, and as a deputy assistant adjutant general there from 1 April 1912 to 18 March 1914. He had two further spells at the War Office, again as a DAAG from 11 December 1918 to 24 January 1919, and as an assistant adjutant general, from 25 January 1919 to 14 February 1920.

Lieutenant Colonel D'Orville Brook Dawson
Officer Commanding, 1st Battalion, Prince of Wales Volunteers
Dawson was born on 2 February 1873, and commissioned from the militia into the South Lancashire Regiment as a 2nd Lieutenant on 2 June 1894. He was promoted to lieutenant on 11 June 1897, to captain on 13 December 1901, and to major on 24 April 1912. He was appointed lieutenant colonel on 28 February 1920.

He served as an adjutant in the militia from 14 March 1908 to 13 March 1911, and as a deputy assistant adjutant and quartermaster general of the South Coast Defences from 27 March 1914 to 4 August 1914.

During World War One, Dawson held the position of assistant adjutant and quartermaster general to the Plymouth Defences from 5 August 1914 to 29 May 1915. He was AA and QMG from 30 May 1915 to 28 June 1916, in the 26th Infantry Division, which was firstly part of the British Expeditionary Force, and then part of the Egyptian Expeditionary Force. He was promoted to assistant quartermaster general, and served with the 12th Army Corps, as part of the EEF and then the British Salonika Force from 29 June 1916 to August 1917. He was AQMG, Eastern Command, 1 February 1918 to 16 September 1918.

Lieutenant Colonel Arthur Derry
Officer Commanding, 1st Battalion, Welch Regiment

Derry was born on 14 October 1874. He was commissioned as a 2nd Lieutenant into the Welch Regiment from the militia on 7 December 1895. Staying with the Welch Regiment, he was promoted lieutenant, 22 April 1898, captain, 9 March 1902, and major on 1 November 1914. He served as battalion adjutant from 11 March 1907 to 10 March 1910. He was appointed lieutenant colonel on 28 November 1920.

Derry served as DAA and QMG of the Welch Division from 1 April 1912 to 22 November 1915. He was AA and QMG of the 53rd Division, Mediterranean Expeditionary Force, from 23 November 1915 to 23 March 1916. Derry served as the brigade major, 115th Infantry Brigade, British armies in France, from 11 July 1916 to 1 April 1917. Towards the end of the World War One, he served as GSO grade 2, with the 57th Division, British armies in France, from 2 April 1917 to 31 July 1917, the 14th Army Corps, British armies in France and the Mediterranean Expeditionary Force, from 1 August 1917 to 24 March 1918, with the 10th Army Corps, British armies in France, from 25 March 1918 to 28 August 1918, and with the 27th Division, British Salonika Force, from 29 August 1918 to 21

November 1918. From 15 May 1919 to 8 November 1919, Derry was the DAA and QMG of the Portsmouth Garrison.

His military awards include the DSO and the OBE.

Lieutenant Colonel William Brooke Thornton
Officer Commanding, 2nd Battalion, Royal Berkshire Regiment
Thornton was born on 30 October 1875, and commissioned into the Royal Berkshire Regiment as a 2nd Lieutenant on 25 March 1896. He remained with the Berkshires and was promoted, lieutenant, 1 May 1899, captain, 8 May 1904, and major on 10 May 1915. He was appointed a lieutenant colonel in the Royal Berkshire Regiment on 13 August 1920.

Thornton served as an adjutant with the militia from 15 February 1905 to 14 February 1908.

During World War One, he was attached to the Egyptian Army from 19 June 1915 to 14 November 1915. He was the battalion commander of the 9th Battalion, Nottinghamshire and Derbyshire Regiment from 23 February 1916 until 13 March 1918. He was made a temporary brigadier general on 3 April 1918, and given command of the 1st Infantry Brigade, British Armies in France, a post he held until 21 September 1918, and was brigade commander of the Irish Reserve Brigade, Home Forces, from 22 September 1918 to 15 April 1919. Again as a temporary lieutenant colonel, he was in charge of the 51st Battalion, Nottinghamshire and Derbyshire Regiment from 16 April 1919 to 6 August 1919.

His military awards include the DSO.

The above information is based on the Army List, January 1921.

APPENDIX C

Biographies of British Officers Killed on Bloody Sunday

THIS INFORMATION IS based on information contained in the personnel files of these officers which are preserved in the National Archives at Kew.

Lieutenant Colonel H.F. Montgomery
Montgomery was a Royal Marine, and was on the GHQ staff in Dublin. During the war, he served with the operations division, the Admirality war staff, London, from, 4 August 1914 to 21 June 1915. From 22 June 1915 to 5 November 1915, he was with the 30th Division at Salisbury. He was in France from 6 November 1915 to 26 March 1919. He was attached to the BAOR before being assigned to Ireland.

He was holder of CMG and DSO.

Major Charles Milne Cholmeley Dowling
Dowling was born on 16 March 1891, and attended Rugby School from 1906 to 1908; after private tuition, he entered Sandhurst on 7 August 1910. He was commissioned as a 2nd Lieutenant into the 2nd Battalion, Grenadier Guards on 9 September 1911, and was promoted lieutenant on 22 March 1913. He left for France with the

2nd Battalion on 12 August 1914.

He was wounded in the hand by shrapnel at Klein Zillebecke on 8 November 1914. He returned to France from medical leave on 10 January 1915, and was promoted captain on 15 July 1915. He again saw service at the front with his new battalion, the 3rd Battalion, Grenadier Guards, and was wounded, at the Hoheuzolleu Redoubt on 16 October 1915. He suffered a severe concussion, brought on by the explosion of an artillery shell. On return to France, he served with both 5th and then 3rd Battalion, Grenadier Guards. Dowling was at this time given some duties in the rear; in later 1916 and through 1917, he acted a railway officer for the Guards Division, as commandant, the Guards Division Area, and as commandant, XIV Corps Area.

However, he was again to see action, and was seriously wounded at Breteucourt on 17 April 1918, and returned to England. He was back in France by July 1918 with the 5th Battalion, Grenadier Guards. After the war, he served in the British Army of the Rhine with the 4th Battalion and then the 2nd Battalion, Grenadier Guards. Dowling returned to England in February 1919, and was appointed acting major in charge of a Dispersal Unit on 17 April 1919.

He resigned from the army on 16 April 1919. He was ordered to remobilise on 30 September 1920, and sent to Ireland.

Captain L. Price

Price was born on 29 August, 1885. Price was a serving reservist with the Honourable Artillery Company; he was a Lance Corporal at the outbreak of World War One. He was commissioned in the field. On 14 December 1915, he joined 20th Battalion, Middlesex Regiment, and by 1917, he was a temporary captain. Price was wounded and listed as missing at Bois Grenier, on 9 April 1918.

Price was mentioned in dispatches twice during the war and awarded the MC. He was listed as being an officer in the Royal Engineers during his service in Dublin.

Captain William Frederick Newberry

Newberry served with the Royal Marine Light Infantry from 1894 to 1895; he then transferred to the 1st Battalion, Royal West Surrey Regiment in which he served until 1908, when he retired with the rank of captain, and moved to Canada. He was educated at Cheltenham College, the Royal Naval College, Greenwich and at Gray's Inn, London. He was registered as a Barrister at Law in both England and Canada, and an expert in military law.

All his service in World War One was on the home front. He commanded a training depot from October 1914 to December 1916. Newberry was the OC of A. Coy of the 18th Battalion, Hampshire Regiment from December 1916, and in 1917 transferred to the position of battalion adjutant with the 6th Battalion, Norfolk Regiment.

He served as an education officer with the 25th Provisional Infantry Brigade, Dublin. But in the casualty list in Appendix II, he is listed as serving with DDHQ RO, which would mean he was a court martial officer, a position consistent with his legal education.

Lieutenant D.L. MacLean

MacLean was born in Ayrshire on 28 August 1889. He was a police constable before enlisting on 22 June 1915, joining the Scots Guards as a private. He was promoted lance corporal, 16 June 1916, made acting corporal, 15 July 1917, and commissioned as a 2nd Lieutenant into the 6th Rifle Brigade on 30 October 1917. He resigned his temporary commission on 10 March 1920, but was recalled and sent to Dublin. MacLean was wounded in the face during World War One.

Lieutenant A. Ames

Peter Ashman Ames was born on 10 June 1888, in Titusville, Pennsylvania, USA. He moved to Morristown, New Jersey, and attended high school there, and also attended Steven's College. He

159

joined the Grenadier Guards, and was commissioned into Guards on 30 March 1917. Ames was discharged at the end of the war, and recalled for special duty in Ireland.

Lieutenant H. Angliss

Angliss was born in Ireland, his service records list both Dublin and Enniskillen as places of birth. His records also list his next of kin, as his mother, Cassie O'Hara, in Kent. Angliss joined the Scottish Rifles in January 1910, and steadily rose through the ranks, becoming a corporal, 19/12/1913, a sergeant 26/6/16, and a CSM on 23/11/16. He was commissioned into 11th Battalion, Royal Inniskilling Fusiliers, on 24/3/1917, from 14th Battalion, Highland Light Infantry.

Angliss was awarded the DCM on 11/12/16. His alias in Dublin was Patrick Mahon.

Cadet F. Garniss

Garniss was serving in the Auxiliary Division, RIC, in Dublin. He first enlisted in 1903, and served in India in 1907/08. He was a labourer and a reservist in RGA before World War One. He re-enlisted in 1914, and again in April 1916 for the period of the war. He was serving as a sergeant with 2nd Battalion, West Yorkshire Regiment, when he was commissioned as a 2nd Lieutenant in the 4th Battalion, Leicestershire Regiment. He was wounded in France in 14 July 1918.

The personal service records were not available for, Captain G.T. Baggallery, Lieutenant R.G. Murray, Lieutenant G. Bennett, Cadet C.A. Morris.

Index